THE TAO OF

BADA BING! SM

DAVID CHASE is an Emmy® Award-winning televison writer, director, and producer whose string of successes includes "The Rockford Files," "I'll Fly Away," and "Northern Exposure."
He is the creator and executive producer of "The Sopranos," for which he writes and directs.

THE TAO OF

BADA BING! ℠

WORDS OF WISDOM FROM

Sopranos ℠

Series Created by David Chase

BRAD GREY
TELEVISION

CH
CARHIL
Carhil Ventures LLC

THE TAO OF BADA BING!
WORDS OF WISDOM FROM THE SOPRANOS
Series Created by David Chase

Copyright © 2003 by Home Box Office, a Division of Time Warner
    Entertainment Company, L.P.

Excerpt from the Introduction by David Chase to *The Sopranos Scriptbook*
    courtesy of Channel 4 Books, an imprint of Pan Macmillan, Ltd.,
    London UK.

Library of Congress CIP data available from the Publisher.

ISBN 1-56649-278-5

ISBN 1-56649-290-4 for the UK/ANZ paperback edition

Printed in the United States by
HAMILTON PRINTING COMPANY

Interior design and composition by
MULBERRY TREE PRESS, INC.
(www.mulberrytreepress.com)

Tao calligraphy © 2003 by Soon Chun Cho

First edition: May 2003
1 3 5 7 9 10 8 6 4 2

Contents

Editors' Note

"What Tony Soprano shows, I guess, is that rarely is
anything black and white in life. Life is difficult, messy,
disappointing. Things don't work out the way we'd like—our
kids make bad choices, our parents are a burden, our friends
disappoint or betray us. In that sense, I hope [*The Sopranos*]
is similar to the foreign films I loved as a young adult for
their ideas, their mystery and their ambiguity."

David Chase
(from the Introduction to *The Sopranos Scriptbook*)

Very little is known about the origins or even the author of the *Tao
Te Ching* (which can be translated as *The Book of the Way* or *the
Path*), the fundamental text of the Chinese philosophy called Taoism.
Nevertheless, the book, presented in 81 brief chapters with no obvi-
ous organizing principle, is a remarkable treatise on life and how to
live it. Not unlike a user's manual, and often written as if intended
to educate or instruct a king or a ruler, it has influenced countless
lives over the past 2,500 years.

The most recognizable symbol attached to Taoism is the yin-yang
symbol. The *yin* represents all that is female and is associated with the
moon, which is dark, passive, cold; its opposite, *yang*, represents the
male and is associated with the sun, which is the light, active, hot
force. According to Taoist beliefs, *yang* contains within it the seed of

yin, just as *yin* contains the seed of *yang*; in addition, all things have both *yin* and *yang* in them, and "from their rise and fall comes new life." The *Tao Te Ching* addresses the constant movement and change of the universe that surrounds us and offers a code of conduct based on moderation and generosity with which to navigate through it.

In the swirling cosmos that is the Garden State, these concepts don't seem so exotic.

Many books in recent times, such as Benjamin Hoff's *The Tao of Pooh*, Fritjof Capra's *The Tao of Physics*, and Bruce Lee's *The Tao of Jeet Kune Do*, have applied Taoist concepts to modern reality. In *The Tao of Bada Bing! Words of Wisdom from The Sopranos*, quotes pulled from the *Tao Te Ching* are juxtaposed against excerpts from all 52 episodes of "The Sopranos," illustrating parallel ideas and themes that appear and reappear throughout the show's four seasons. For instance, "Thirty Spokes Converge" conveys the organization and responsibilities of the Mafia family. "Yin-Yang" considers the place of women. "My Sustenance Comes from the Mother" examines Tony's troubled relationship with his mother, Livia. "An Excessive Love" shows just how dangerous our desires and needs can be. "The Highest Type of Ruler," "You Fight a War by Exceptional Moves," and "The Best Way of Employing a Man" emphasize the inherent contradictions and complexities of being—and working for—a Mob boss; and so on.

The rewards and tribulations of daily existence, how to give and get respect, striking a balance between what you want from others and what they want from you—such paradoxes are faced by the Tony Soprano in all of us. As David Chase, creator of "The Sopranos," says, nothing in life is black and white. The meaning of life is to be found in the ebb and flow between the two—not a bad way to describe the Tao.

John Weber and Chuck Kim

THE TAO OF

BADA BING!

Thirty Spokes Converge

Thirty spokes converge upon a single hub;
It is on the hole in the center that the use of the cart hinges.

Tao Te Ching ☯ 11

TONY: All right, you know why we're here. So if you've got any
doubts or reservations, now is the time to say so. No one will
think any less of you. Because once you enter this family, there's
no getting out. This family comes before everything else . . .
Everything. Before your wife and your children and your mother
and your father. It's a thing of honor. And, God forbid, if you get
sick or something happens and you can't earn, we'll take care of
you. 'Cause that's part of it.

PAULIE: If you got a problem, you just gotta let somebody know. This
man right here. He's like your father. It doesn't matter if it's with
somebody here or on the outside. You bring it to him, he'll solve it.

TONY: You stay within the family. All right, give me your hand. Okay.
[TONY AND CHRISTOPHER PRICK FINGERS. TONY BURNS TWO
ST. PETER CARDS.] That's St. Peter, my family saint. Now, as that
card burns, so may your soul burn in hell if you betray your friends

in the family. Now rub your hands together like this and repeat after me. May I burn in hell . . .

EUGENE AND CHRISTOPHER: May I burn in hell . . .

TONY: If I betray my friends.

EUGENE AND CHRISTOPHER: If I betray my friends.

TONY: Congratulations.

(Season 3, Episode 3, "Fortunate Son")

PAULIE: You're a made guy now. It's your turn to make some real money and I get to relax a little. Your only problem in life now is you give me ten points of your take every settle-up day. Other than that, you got no problem. My only problem in life? I gotta kick my points to that man over there. And onward goes this thing of ours. When you think of all the headaches most human beings have in life . . . ours are all boiled down to only one. Not a bad deal, huh?

CHRISTOPHER: You got it.

PAULIE: Only thing: there's a six G minimum every week. I gotta get something outta this. But six grand, that could be a lot or a little. Depends on you and how much you grow the business.

CHRISTOPHER: You got it . . . I love you, Paulie. We're in it together now.

PAULIE: I love you too, kid.

(Season 3, Episode 3, "Fortunate Son")

TONY: I wanna know why there's zero growth in this family's re-ceipts. You're supposed to be earners. That's why you got the top tier positions. So each one a you go out to your people on the street, crack some fuckin' heads . . . create some fuckin' earners out there! My uncle . . . The boss of this family, is on trial for his life. And what you people are kickin' up there is a fuckin' disgrace. You know how much lawyers cost? A major RICO like his? I'm the only one supportin' him. This thing is a pyramid, since time immemorial. Shit runs downhill, money goes up. It's that simple. I should not have to be comin' here, hat in my hand, remindin' you about your duty to that man. And I don't wanna hear about the fuckin' economy either! I don't wanna hear it. Sil, break it down for 'em. What two businesses have traditionally been recession-proof since time immemorial?

SILVIO: Certain aspects of show business, and our thing.

TONY: Now that's it. That's all I gotta say.

(Season 4, Episode 1, "For All Debts Public and Private")

Yin-Yang

Tao gave birth to One,
One gave birth to Two,
Two gave birth to Three,
Three gave birth to all the myriad things.
All the myriad things carry the Yin on
Their backs and hold the Yang in their embrace.

Tao Te Ching ☯ 42

The feminine can always conquer the masculine by yielding.

Tao Te Ching ☯ 61

LIVIA: Well, all I know is, daughters are much better at takin' care of their mothers than sons.

(Season 1, Episode 1, "Pilot")

TONY: Now that my father's dead, he's a saint. When he was alive, nothin'. My dad was tough, he ran his own crew. A guy like that and my mother wore him down to a little nub. He was a squeakin' gerbil when he died.

DR. MELFI: Quite a formidable maternal presence.

(Season 1, Episode 1, "Pilot")

TONY: Remember the Alatore's, Ma?

LIVIA: Oh, why wouldn't I? You know, they moved to Nevada. They're millionaires now. Oh, that Rocco Alatore, he was a real go-getter.

TONY: Didn't Dad wanna go with him?

LIVIA: Your father? No.

TONY: Yeah, he did. I remember you guys talkin' about it. Alatore was gonna start a business, Dad was gonna do a little thing with him.

LIVIA: Oh, well Rocco just got him all worked up, that's all. What is this, with all these questions?

TONY: Dad wanted to go with him. You wouldn't let him.

LIVIA: Let him?

TONY: M–hm.

LIVIA: What do ya mean? You just tell me one time your father didn't do exactly as he wanted.

TONY: I don't know. Maybe this was his chance to get out. I know Dad was no choir boy, but maybe with a little bit of support, ya know?

LIVIA: Oh, Mr. Sensitive, now. Well, if it bothers you, maybe you better talk to a psychiatrist!

TONY: Whoa, what are you talkin' about, a psychiatrist?

LIVIA: Well that's what people do when they're looking for somebody to blame for their life, isn't it?

TONY: You're a real stone player, aren't you Ma? You threatening to smother your children!

LIVIA: What does that mean?

TONY: You know, everybody thought Dad was the ruthless one, but I gotta hand it to you. If you'd been born after those feminists, you woulda been the real gangster.

LIVIA: I don't know what you're talkin' about!

(Season 1, Episode 7, "Down Neck")

ANNALISA: What can I do for you?

TONY: Well you could introduce me to the boss.

ANNALISA: You can talk to me.

TONY: A fucking *woman* boss?!

ANNALISA: So what do you want?

TONY: Never happen in the States, never.

ANNALISA: Our men kill each other. All my brothers, for example, they all got murdered. Or they go to prison. Rome has a war against us. But the men are in love to their mama, huh? So, obeying a woman, is not, como se dice? It comes natural, huh?

TONY: Well I'll be dipped in shit. You go around like your father's nursemaid.

ANNALISA: I am my father's nursemaid.

TONY: Well if an old man carries the respect of the troops, you keep him around. I did something like that myself.

ANNALISA: We are cousins.

(Season 2, Episode 4, "Commendatori")

CARMELA: Joan, hi. Is this a bad time?

JOAN: Always. Come on in.

CARMELA: [HANDS JOAN A PIE] Ricotta pie with pineapples.

JOAN: Oh, wow.

CARMELA: I was in the neighborhood. My mother's foot surgeon is over here.

JOAN: Oh, thank you. Listen, Carmela, I think I know why you're here. My sister told me that you wanted me to write a letter to Georgetown for uh . . . Fielder, is it?

CARMELA: Uh, Meadow.

JOAN: Oh, I'm sorry. But I just can't do it.

CARMELA: Well, I thought you would at least want to take a look at her grades and her SAT scores. And some teacher comments before you made up your mind. I think she would be a wonderful addition to the Georgetown campus.

JOAN: Then I'm sure the admissions offices will see that.

CARMELA: Well, I'm not sure that's true. The sad fact is that's just not enough these days.

JOAN: I'm sorry, Carmela. But I can't do it.

CARMELA: I don't think you understand. I want you to write that letter.

JOAN: Excuse me?

CARMELA: I said I want you to write the letter.

JOAN: Are you threatening me?

CARMELA: Threat? What threatening? I brought you a ricotta pie, and a high school transcript so you could write a letter of recommendation for my little daughter to Georgetown.

JOAN: I'm an officer of the court.

CARMELA: A lawyer. [LAUGHS] Don't make me beg here.

JOAN: I've already written my last letter of support for this academic year.

CARMELA: Well, how about this. I thought you could write a letter to Georgetown, tell them that you've discovered that Georgetown was not that person's first choice . . . and that in fact he was using Georgetown as a backup. I'm not gonna tell you what to write. [SETS AN ENVELOPE ON JOAN'S DESK] Oh, my God, I left my mother in the car with that foot. Thanks for this.

(Season 2, Episode 8, "Full Leather Jacket")

ROSALIE: Speaking of grandkids, I am just sick about Jackie and Meadow. I asked him what happened, he tells me to mind my own business.

CARMELA: Well so does she in so many words.

ANGIE: They broke up? Is Meadow okay?

CARMELA: Oh, please. That girl is so different than I was at her age. Just rolls off her back. No weight loss. No sleepless nights.

GABRIELLA: Not like the grief we go through with our husbands.

ANGIE: That's 'cause we married these walyos.

ROSALIE: It's not just us. The President of the United States for cryin' out loud? I mean look what his wife had to put up with the blow jobs and the stained dress.

ANGIE: Hillary Clinton? I can't stand that woman.

ROSALIE: I don't know. Maybe we could all take a page from her book.

CARMELA: What, to be humiliated in public and then walk around smiling all the time? That is *so false*. I would dig a hole, I would climb into it and I would not come out.

ROSALIE: All I know is, she stuck by him and put up with the bullshit and in the end . . . what'd she do? She set up her own little thing.

GABRIELLA: She did. She took all that negative shit he gave her, spun it into gold. You gotta give her credit.

CARMELA: That's true, isn't it? She's a role model for all of us.

(Season 3, Episode 12, "Amour Fou")

The Journey of a Thousand Miles

The journey of a thousand miles
Begins with a single step.

Tao Te Ching ☯ **64**

DR. MELFI: Anthony, what is it you want to achieve here?

TONY: What do I want to achieve? I wanna stop passin' out. I wanna stop fuckin' panickin'. I wanna direct my power and my fuckin' anger against the people in my life that deserve it. I want to be in total control.

DR. MELFI: There's no such thing as total control.

TONY: Of course there is.

(Season 2, Episode 5, "Big Girls Don't Cry")

TONY: Try to keep a low profile and what's the fuckin' point? I'm still a miserable prick and I'm still passing out. Thing on the History

Channel the other night on the American Revolution. You know we're the only country in the world where the pursuit of happiness is guaranteed in writing? Do you believe that? Hm? Bunch of fuckin' spoiled brats. Where's my happiness then?

DR. MELFI: It's the pursuit that guaranteed.

TONY: Yeah, always a fuckin' loophole. Right?

(Season 2, Episode 11, "House Arrest")

TONY: See, that's what's wrong with the world, right there. An innocent person is driving along, minding their own business, and some fuckin' asshole comes out and smashes into 'em.

DR. MELFI: You can't control everything that happens.

TONY: But you can get pissed off.

DR. MELFI: And then what? Lose control?

TONY: Who said anything about that? You direct your anger where it belongs.

DR. MELFI: You have panic attacks. Panic occurs when feelings of anger, revenge, whatever, overwhelm you. That's where behavioral therapy comes in. It can teach you to control those triggers.

TONY: Then how do you get people to do what you want?

(Season 3, Episode 4, "Employee of the Month")

DR. MELFI: What else is going on? How was the rest of your week?

TONY: To be honest, very good.

DR. MELFI: Why is that?

TONY: Well, that's how life is I guess. Sometimes it's good, sometimes it's bad. Things come, things go.

DR. MELFI: How are things between you and Carmela?

TONY: She was moody for a little while but now she's her old self. Maybe it was coming here.

DR. MELFI: Possibly. Well, you do look happy I must say.

TONY: Yeah . . . Went to the zoo the other day . . .

DR. MELFI: The zoo?

TONY: Mm—hm. You know sometimes you gotta get away, and stop and smell the gorilla shit. It's good to be in nature though.

DR. MELFI: And the zoo made you happy?

TONY: Yeah . . . I think a lot of it's 'cause of you too. You put a lot of time into me, and now it's payin' off.

DR. MELFI: The progress that you make is entirely up to you, and how willing you are to be honest with yourself and with me.

TONY: Well I am improving. You have to joyfully participate in the suffering of the world.

DR. MELFI: Your thoughts have a kind of Eastern flavor to them.

TONY: Well, I've lived in Jersey my whole life.

(Season 3, Episode 9, "The Telltale Moozadell")

DOMINIC: [ABOUT CHRISTOPHER] Paul? You wanna read your statement?

PAULIE: I don't write nothin' down. So I'll keep this short and sweet. You're weak. You're outta control. And you've become an embarrassment to yourself and everybody else.

CHRISTOPHER: Ho-ho, listen to you.

DOMINIC: Guys, guys. Whoa, whoa, whoa. We said, "non-judgmental."

PAULIE: Fuck that. Let him take his medicine.

CHRISTOPHER: Seriously, Paulie, you wanna talk about fuckin' up?

PAULIE: Watch it, Chrissy.

CHRISTOPHER: What? I thought we're bein' honest here. You got some balls, you know that? All a you. You want to talk about self-control—how about you, Sil? Fuckin' every slut you got workin' in the place when you got a wife and kids at home.

DOMINIC: Guys, guys. Whoa, whoa.

ADRIANA: Christopher.

CHRISTOPHER: Or you, Paulie. Yeah, remember last winter in the woods with the Russian guy.

TONY: Christopher, I am fuckin' warnin' you!

CHRISTOPHER: There he goes, Mr. Type A Personality.

TONY: We are here to talk about you killin' yourself with drugs! Not my fuckin' personality!

DOMINIC: That's right.

CHRISTOPHER: I'm gonna kill myself? The way you fuckin' eat you're gonna have a heart attack by the time you're fifty.

DOMINIC: Paulie, sit down.

PAULIE: You're talkin' to the boss here.

JOANNE: Good, maybe someone will knock some goddamn sense into him!

CHRISTOPHER: Great, my own mother. Fuck you, you fuckin' whore!

(Season 4, Episode 10, "The Strong, Silent Type")

TONY: Which one of the twelve steps you on now?

CHRISTOPHER: The only one I haven't exactly done is go around to all the people I fucked over while I was using and apologize.

TONY: Maybe you shouldn't do that one. You know, let sleepin' dogs lie.

CHRISTOPHER: That's what I was thinking. Maybe in a couple of cases, I'll send flowers. Or cash, in some cases.

(Season 4, Episode 13, "Whitecaps")

Written in the Blood

Every being in the universe
Is an expression of the Tao.
It springs into existence,
Unconscious, perfect, free,
Takes on a physical body,
Lets circumstances complete it.
That is why every being
Spontaneously honors the Tao.

Tao Te Ching ☯ 51

To accept destiny is to face life with open eyes.
Not to accept destiny is to face death blindfold.

Tao Te Ching ☯ 16

TONY: You know, I put food on the table. My father was in it, my uncle was in it. Maybe I was too lazy to think for myself. Consider myself a rebel.

(Season 1, Episode 5, "College")

CHRISTOPHER: Yo.

TONY: What have you got?

CHRISTOPHER: Wet shoes.

TONY: Hey, you chose this life, you don't wanna work in the rain, try out for the fuckin' Yankees.

(Season 1, Episode 5, "College")

CARMELA: Forgive me, Father, for I have sinned. It has been four weeks since my last confession—what am I talkin' about? That's a lie. I haven't truly confessed in twenty years.

FATHER PHIL: Go on.

CARMELA: I have forsaken what is right for what is easy. Allowing what I know is evil in my house. Allowing my children, oh my God, my sweet children to be a part of it. Because I wanted things for them. Wanted a better life. Good schools. I wanted this house. I wanted money in my hands, money to buy anything I ever wanted. I'm so ashamed. My husband . . . I think he has committed horrible acts. I think he has . . . well, you know all about him, Father Phil. I'm the same, I've said nothing, I've done nothing about it. I got a bad feeling. It's just a matter of time before God compensates me with outrage for my sins.

(Season 1, Episode 5, "College")

LIVIA: [ABOUT ANTHONY JR.] It's a crime! To suspend that child from school with all the money you give them?!

JUNIOR: I bet that gym teacher shit a brick when your little friend puked on his boots, huh, Anthony?

[ANTHONY JR. LAUGHS]

TONY: Wanna encourage him, Uncle Jun?

JUNIOR: Hey, whatever happened to "boys will be boys"?

CARMELA: He stole from the church. They don't make 'em any lower than that.

MEADOW: What a loser.

CARMELA: That's enough outta you.

LIVIA: Oh, his father was the same way. I practically lived in that vice principal's office.

TONY: Could we not, please?

LIVIA: Oh, you only remember what you wanna remember! Yeah, well I must've had another son who stole a car when he was ten years old. Yeah, he could barely see over the steering wheel.

JUNIOR: He was a hellion, this one. Him and his little crew, they used to steal lobsters from the boats on the shore and sell 'em for a buck apiece down on Bloomfield Avenue.

ANTHONY JR.: Really?

TONY: How many times do I gotta say this?! I don't want that kinda talk in front of this kid. That stuff is wrong and I don't condone it!

(Season 1, Episode 7, "Down Neck")

TONY: My son is doomed, right?

DR. MELFI: Why do you say that?

TONY: Come on. This is the part where I'm supposed to tell you how terrible my father was, and the terrible things he did to me, and how he ruined my life! But I'll tell ya somethin', I was proud to be Johnny Soprano's kid! When he beat the shit outta that guy, I went to the class, I told them how tough my father was!

DR. MELFI: Do you think that's how your son feels about you?

TONY: Yeah, probably! And I'm glad, I'm glad if he's proud of me. But that's the bind I'm in, 'cause I don't want him to *be* like me! He could be anything he wants to be.

⊕   ⊕   ⊕   ⊕   ⊕*

DR. MELFI: Have you communicated any of this to your son?

TONY: Not in so many words. Probably not at all. And what difference would it make? You said so yourself. It's in the blood. It's hereditary.

DR. MELFI: Genetic predispositions are only that, predispositions. It's not a destiny written in stone. People have choices!

TONY: She finally offers an opinion.

DR. MELFI: Well, they do. You think that everything that happens is preordained? You don't think that human beings possess free will?

TONY: How come I'm not makin' fuckin' pots in Peru? You're born into this shit! You are what you are!

(Season 1, Episode 7, "Down Neck")

---

*Denotes a deletion of a portion of the script.

PUSSY: What's the matter?

TONY: That kid. He used to be happy-go-lucky, you know. Now he's moody, he questions the fuckin' universe.

PUSSY: Hey, Ton, like father like son, huh?

(Season 2, Episode 7, "D-Girl")

CARMELA: Gentle and merciful Lord Jesus. I want to speak to you now with an open heart, with an honest heart. Tonight I ask you to take my sins and the sins of my family into your merciful heart. We have chosen this life in full awareness of the consequences of our sins. I know that Christopher's life is in your hands. And his fate is your will. I ask you humbly to spare him. And if it is your will to spare him, I ask that you deliver him from blindness and grant him vision. And through this vision, may he see your love . . . and gain the strength to carry on in service to your mercy. In the name of the Father and the Son and the Holy Spirit.

(Season 2, Episode 9, "From Where to Eternity")

DAVID: You told me not to get in the game. Why'd you let me do it?

TONY: Well, I knew you had this business here, Davey. It's my nature. The Frog and the Scorpion, you know. And besides if you woulda won I'd be the one cryin' the blues, right?

DAVID: What's the end?

TONY: The end? It's . . . planned bankruptcy. Hey, you're not the first guy to get busted out. This is how a guy like me makes a livin'.

This is my bread and butter. When this is over, you're free to go. You can go anywhere you want.

(Season 2, Episode 10, "Bust Out")

MACKENZIE: So, Mead, was he dealing while you guys were dating?

KELLI: Hey, Mackenzie . . . why don't you shut your fuckin' mouth?

MACKENZIE: I was just asking.

KELLI: Oh, please. Okay? My brother's whole stupid pathetic dream was to follow in our father's footsteps. What, I gotta paint a picture? He was killed by some fat fuck in see-through socks. Take your pick, they all look alike.

MEADOW: Actually, Kelli, you really have no basis to say that.

KELLI: We used to joke around about our families. What happened to you?

MEADOW: Look, I know this is a really painful time for you, but your brother's best friend was an Israeli X dealer. I met him.

KELLI: Wow! So, it was international.

MEADOW: Let's just drop it, okay?

KELLI: Yeah, right. I mean, if my dad still controlled all the crime in north Jersey like your dad does now, I'd probably want to drop it, too. But then, it might not have happened.

MEADOW: Wait, this is way beyond. Our dads are in the garbage business. And it's always good for a laugh and, yeah, they brush up against organized crime. But you think they control every slimeball and illegal gun in like a hundred communities? The fact that you would even say this in front of an outsider is amazing to me. Jesus Christ, some loyalty?

(Season 3, Episode 13, "The Army of One")

TONY: Been wantin' to talk to you.

CHRISTOPHER: Yeah, been wantin' to talk to you, too.

TONY: I'll go first. I gotta make it my number one priority . . . to limit my exposure to potentially damagin' conversations and wiretap shit like that.

CHRISTOPHER: Sure. A guy in your position . . .

TONY: So . . . over the next coupla years, more and more, I'm gonna be givin' my orders through you. And then finally . . . only through you.

CHRISTOPHER: Well, what about Sil? You got that with him, and Paulie.

TONY: Those other guys, Sil, Paulie . . . one thing they're not . . . they're not my blood. You hear what I'm sayin' to you? It's a matter of trust.

CHRISTOPHER: It's very wise.

TONY: Sil's a good consiglieri, he's gonna continue on as such but he's no fuckin' spring chicken, either. But on the other hand it's no reason to be givin' him a fuckin' attitude.

CHRISTOPHER: *No.* Of course not.

TONY: Now there's gonna be a period of transition.

CHRISTOPHER: Jesus Christ, T.

TONY: You're gonna take this family into the twenty-first century.

CHRISTOPHER: We're already in the twenty-first century though, T. Whatever you say, T. I'd follow you into the gates of hell. That's what I was gonna say to you. What you did for me, that fuck who killed my father. I'll never forget that. I only hope I'm worthy.

TONY: Why wouldn't you be worthy?

(Season 4, Episode 6, "Everybody Hurts")

ARTIE: But you don't understand. The money's gone.

TONY: Can't you come and talk to me? Hey. Hey, I'm your friend. Suppose you hadn't been able to reach me and I come over to your house and I find you're dead. How am I s'pposed to feel?

ARTIE: Take the restaurant.

TONY: I don't want the fuckin' restaurant.

ARTIE: Then how am I gonna pay you back? Fifty thousand dollars, it'll take the rest of my life.

TONY: Well it's fifty-one-five, vig-wise, Artie, and . . . technically you already missed a payment. [ARTIE CRYING, MOANS] All right look, let's just . . . we'll wipe my tab at the restaurant.

ARTIE: Thank you. But Tony, that's what? Six thousand dollars. What about the rest of the money?

TONY: I'll assume the guy's debt. Collect the fifty G's.

ARTIE: Thank you. The cobwebs are now removed.

TONY: The fuck are you talkin' about?

ARTIE: You saw this whole thing, didn't you? You knew exactly what was gonna happen. You can see twenty moves down the road. Please, I don't blame you — I envy you. It's like an instinct. Like a hawk sees a little mouse movin' around a cornfield from a mile up.

TONY: You think it's *my* fault you're fuckin' lyin' in here?

ARTIE: It's just that somebody mentions fifty grand to bankroll a French digestif and your mind goes through all the permutations at like Internet speed and realizes, ho . . . worst case scenario . . . I eat for free.

TONY: You fuckin' suicide! You're disgraceful!

(Season 4, Episode 6, "Everybody Hurts")

My Sustenance Comes from the Mother

Everyone else takes his place and does his job;
I alone remain natural and free.
I am different from others; my sustenance
Comes directly from the Mother.

Tao Te Ching ☯ 20

JUNIOR: What's goin' on? My Dominican girl said you called me.

LIVIA: Well . . . he sold our house.

JUNIOR: Don't people have names anymore? Who's "he"?

LIVIA: Anthony. He sold my house! The home my husband and I made!

JUNIOR: What else were they gonna do with it?

LIVIA: You too!

JUNIOR: Hey!

LIVIA: I suppose he would've found it harder to have his meetings at my house, than in this nursing home.

JUNIOR: What are you talkin' about, meetings?

LIVIA: Don't think I'll ever see any of that money, either.

JUNIOR: What meetings?

LIVIA: Raymond, Larry! That sneak from Manhattan.

JUNIOR: Johnny Sack? Johnny Sack was here?

LIVIA: With his mohair suits and his shoe lifts.

JUNIOR: Suits, pleurisy? More than once he was here? Why didn't I know about this?

LIVIA: Well, maybe it was you they were talking about, who knows? Well, I just don't like being put in the middle of things! I shoulda known something was strange when suddenly Larry Boy's mother moved in here. And then Jimmy Altieri's mother.

JUNIOR: Three of my capos have their mothers in this place?

LIVIA: Instead of living in normal homes with their sons, like human beings.

JUNIOR: This must be some kind of fuckin' end move. What do they think, I'm stupid? We'll see!

LIVIA: Now, wait a minute! I don't like that kind of talk! Now just stop it, it upsets me! Or I won't tell you anything anymore.

JUNIOR: If this is true, Livia, you know what I mean . . . I'm the boss for Pete's sake! If I don't act, blood or no . . . I *have* to.

LIVIA: Oh, God! What, what did I say now? I suppose I shoulda just kept my mouth shut, like a mute. And then everybody would've been happy.

(Season 1, Episode 11, "Nobody Knows Anything")

TONY: [CRYING] I had lunch with that girl next door, ya know.

MELFI: You did?

TONY: Isabella. She was tellin' me about the Avellino, where my people are from. It sounded nice. Anyway, she was talkin', and all of a sudden . . . ya know, uh, we went to another place, like, in my mind's eye. I don't know, we went back in time to like 1907 or somethin'. And we were in this room, you know, and she had this baby, she was holdin' it, you know, on her breast, she was nursin' it. She was whisperin' to it, like, "It's okay, little baby, don't cry, it's gonna be okay, I love you."

MELFI: Did the baby have a name?

TONY: She was callin' it Antonio.

MELFI: Anthony, your fantasy, that's you, that little baby. And Isabella, she was nursing you.

TONY: Oh, fuck me.

(Season 1, Episode 12, "Isabella")

TONY: I gotta talk to you.

MELFI: What's wrong?

TONY: There was no Isabella.

MELFI: What?!

TONY: There was no Isabella, I just talked to Cusamano, him and the whosits just got back from Bermuda, I asked him, "Where's the dental exchange student that's stayin' at your house?" He looked at me like I was fuckin' oobatz.

MELFI: But you said that your wife saw her, that you both argued about it.

TONY: Yeah, I asked her about that.

MELFI: And?

TONY: You thought she was pissed then? You should see her now, now that I told her the whole thing was just a fantasy.

MELFI: Discontinue the Lithium.

TONY: I already flushed it.

MELFI: Even if it was the medicine, this fantasy of yours has meaning. You know, the issue of mother and child, the Madonna.

TONY: Excuse, me, you didn't see this broad.

MELFI: Did you ever flirt or come-on sexually with Isabella?

TONY: No.

MELFI: Why not? You said she was very beautiful and voluptuous? Another question. Why now?

TONY: What d'ya mean?

MELFI: Why the need for the fantasy of a loving, caring woman now?

TONY: I don't know.

MELFI: I think you should come in so we could talk face to face.

TONY: I can't right now.

MELFI: You know, your mother is always talking about infanticide.

TONY: Yeah, it's a sad situation that goes on in the world.

MELFI: Are you still feeling okay?

TONY: I feel pretty good, actually. When I find out who took a shot at me, I'm gonna feel even better.

(Season 1, Episode 12, "Isabella")

DR. MELFI: Isn't it interesting how this memory loss has cropped up, right after you failed to be killed in the carjacking? You think it was a carjacking?

TONY: Of course not! But I got an idea who was behind it, and . . . enough said. You don't wanna go there.

DR. MELFI: Maybe you don't wanna go there.

TONY: What are you talkin' about?

DR. MELFI: Well, let's track it. Right around the time of the shooting, you were having hallucinations of that Isabella figure? The protective, loving mother? Your subconscious was shouting something at you. On the day before the shooting, you said to me that she kept going on, and yet again about news stories of mothers throwing their babies out of windows.

TONY: Oh, why don't we put our fuckin' cards on the table here! What, what do you think, my mother tried to have me whacked 'cause I put her in a nursing home?

DR. MELFI: In your worst dreams, a duck flies off with your penis! Castration!

TONY: Hey, my mother never went after my basket.

DR. MELFI: No, not literally. Look, ordinarily a patient is helped to make his own breakthroughs. But your life is in danger, so okay, I'm willing to put the cards on the table. I say what your mother has, at the very least is what we call Borderline Personality Disorder.

TONY: A Borderline Personality Disorder?

DR. MELFI: Lemme read to you from the DSM form, okay? Definitions of the condition. "A pattern of unstable relationships, effective instability." It means intense anxiety, a joylessness. These people's internal phobias are the only things that exist to them, the real world, real people are peripheral. These people have no love or compassion. Borderline personalities are very good at splitting behavior, creating bitterness and conflict between others in their circle.

TONY: You twisted fuckin' bitch! That's my mother we're talkin' about, not some fuck up in Attica, stabbin' you in the shower!

DR. MELFI: Relax.

TONY: See we're through, you and I. We're finished. And you're lucky if I don't break your fuckin' face in fifty thousand pieces!

DR. MELFI: Okay.

(Season 1, Episode 13, "I Dream of Jeannie Cusamano")

LIVIA: You're a good boy, Arthur. Comin' to visit me.

ARTIE: We go back a ways. You made a mean PB & J.

LIVIA: After what my son did to you. Oh, how can I look you in the face?

ARTIE: Tony? What did he do now?

LIVIA: You don't blame him for setting the fire? Well, you're a bigger man than some. Well we should all be grateful that nobody was incinerated to death.

(Season 1, Episode 13, "I Dream of Jeannie Cusamano")

CARMELA: Here, one a mine. It'll help you sleep.

TONY: What kinda person can I be, where his own mother wants him dead?

CARMELA: The problem is not with you. That woman is a peculiar duck, she always has been.

TONY: Yeah, but that's not the point.

CARMELA: No, and she's gotten worse with age. You think my mother didn't warn me about her on my wedding night?

TONY: Please, don't start with that again.

CARMELA: Both your sisters left New Jersey so young, you woulda thought there were contracts out on them.

TONY: I know.

CARMELA: But you were different. You tried to make it work.

TONY: Two pricks with nine millimeters . . . my self-esteem is non-existent right now.

CARMELA: I could kill her. With these two hands. The next time I see her, it's gonna be . . .

TONY: You gotta play the concerned daughter-in-law, you gotta stay even-keeled, for the sake of the business.

CARMELA: Fuck the business. And lemme tell you somethin', Tony, dollars to donuts, this Alzheimer's thing is an act, so she can't be called on her shit!

TONY: Uncle Jun and I, we had our problems, with the business, but I never shoulda razzed him about eatin' pussy. This whole war coulda been averted. Cunnilingus and psychiatry brought us to this.

CARMELA: You *had* to see a shrink because of the mother you had.

(Season 1, Episode 13, "I Dream of Jeannie Cusamano")

FATHER PHIL: Art! Hello, how are things?

ARTIE: Good, Father. Busy.

FATHER PHIL: Yeah?

ARTIE: You?

FATHER PHIL: Like the man said . . . "Rust never sleeps."

ARTIE: Listen, Father, I wanna thank you for takin' the time out to talk to me the other day.

FATHER PHIL: Did you bring your wife into things?

ARTIE: No.

FATHER PHIL: No?

ARTIE: Sitting there, in the house of God, I realized . . . You can either be a *yes* person or a *no* person. A *positive* ion, or a *negative* ion.

FATHER PHIL: I'm not quite sure I get what you're saying.

ARTIE: [ABOUT LIVIA] It's just that, this woman's always been an odd bird, a sea of negativity. Even as a kid, we all learned to take her ravings with a grain of salt.

FATHER PHIL: But you also said the *son* was unstable.

ARTIE: I was . . . angry. Complicated, yes he is. A little too comfortable outside the law, yes he is. But it would only add to the quotient of sorrow in the world to doubt him. When the source, unfortunately, is a person who rarely has a kind word for anyone.

(Season 1, Episode 13, "I Dream of Jeannie Cusamano")

DR. MELFI: Anthony, I think it's important we talk about your mother and what she tried to do to you.

TONY: Don't need to. She showed her true colors, that's all.

DR. MELFI: Has Anthony Jr. heard you say, "She's dead to me?"

TONY: I don't know.

DR. MELFI: Well, don't you think that that kind of talk could lead a kid to embrace these ideas?

TONY: Oh, so now this is my fault?

DR. MELFI: No. When some people first realize that they're solely responsible for their decisions, actions and beliefs and that death lies at the end of every road . . . they can be overcome with intense dread.

TONY: Intense dread?

DR. MELFI: A dull aching anger that leads them to conclude that the only absolute truth . . . is death.

TONY: I think the kid's onto somethin'.

(Season 2, Episode 7, "D-Girl")

TONY: [ABOUT GLORIA] She *wanted* me to fuckin' kill her.

DR. MELFI: Like suicide by cop.

TONY: So she set me up? From the beginning, Gloria saw me as only a fuckin' hammer?

DR. MELFI: She loved you.

TONY: She looked so good, too, that day in your office. Just another Irina with a college degree.

DR. MELFI: Ask yourself. How did you recognize in Gloria, underneath all her layers of sophistication . . . this deeply wounded . . . angry being that would let you replicate once again your relationship with your mother.

TONY: I don't wanna fuck my mother. I don't give a shit what you say, you're never gonna convince me.

DR. MELFI: Not fuck . . . try to please her. Try to win her love.

TONY: Forty fuckin' years old.

DR. MELFI: We need to repeat what's familiar, even if it's bad for us. Gloria's need for drama. The selfishness. The incessant self-regard. At one time . . . in your mother's hands, it passed for love.

(Season 3, Episode 12, "Amour Fou")

DR. KOBLER: You don't like talking much about Dad, do you?

MEADOW: It doesn't bother me.

DR. KOBLER: Meadow, I'm gonna ask you a question about Dad. This may be very painful for you. Did Dad ever molest you?

MEADOW: No.

DR. KOBLER: I don't tell them what we discuss, Meadow.

MEADOW: Yeah, I don't think so.

DR. KOBLER: What about Mom?

MEADOW: God no. Unless you consider obsessing about my fucking GPA an assault, which I do.

(Season 4, Episode 2, "No-Show")

Those Who Know

Those who know don't talk.
Those who talk don't know.

Tao Te Ching ☯ 56

DR. MELFI: Anxiety attacks are legitimate psychiatric emergencies. Suppose you were driving and you passed out.

TONY: Let me tell you somethin'. Nowadays everybody's gotta go to shrinks and counselors and go on Sally Jesse Raphael and talk about their problems. What ever happened to . . . Gary Cooper? The strong silent type? *That* was an American. He wasn't in touch with his feelin's. He just did what he had to do. See, see what they didn't know was once they got Gary Cooper in touch with his feelin's, that they wouldn't be able to shut him up! And then it's dysfunction this and dysfunction that, and dysfunction vafungol!

(Season 1, Episode 1, "Pilot")

FATHER PHIL: You know what's remarkable . . . If you take everything Jesus ever said, add it up, it only amounts to two hours of talk.

CARMELA: No?

FATHER PHIL: Um–hmm.

CARMELA: No, but wait. I heard the same thing about the Beatles. Except it was if you add up all their songs it only comes to ten hours.

(Season 1, Episode 5, "College")

TONY: About four or five months ago I started seeing a psychiatrist. You know, I was passin' out and they couldn't find nothin'. She's been helpin' me with that. Okay, come on, give it to me. Give it to my face, come on!

SILVIO: [ABOUT TONY'S THERAPY] Well, I'm sure you did it with complete . . . discretion. And, uh, speakin' for Pussy, if he's still alive, I'm sure he would agree.

TONY: Business was not discussed, no names were mentioned. Junior knows. He's decided to use it against me. Ask now, 'cause we're not discussin' this again.

PAULIE: It's not the worst thing I ever heard. I was seein' a therapist myself about a year ago. I had some issues, enough said. I learned some copin' skills.

SILVIO: Look, this thing of ours, the way it's goin', be better if we could admit to each other, these are painful, stressful times. But it'll never fuckin' happen.

TONY: [TO CHRISTOPHER] What about you. You gotta problem with this?

CHRISTOPHER: Um . . . what is it, like, marriage counseling?

TONY: Yeah, like that. Sorta, yeah.

(Season 1, Episode 13, "I Dream of Jeannie Cusamano")

DR. MELFI: Anthony's attacks, how do they make you feel?

CARMELA: Well, concerned of course, helpless . . . a little frustrated maybe.

DR. MELFI: You mean with your inability to help him.

CARMELA: Uh, no. To tell the truth, I was referring to your inability to help him.

TONY: She has helped me. What are you talkin' about?

CARMELA: You've been coming here for three years, Tony, and you still pass out on a regular basis.

DR. MELFI: I understand your frustration . . . . did Anthony share with you any of our insights about his last panic attack?

TONY: I told you, remember? The gabagool, my mother when I was a kid.

CARMELA: Right. Yes.

DR. MELFI: Do you think that there is anything in the present family dynamic that could serve as a trigger? Something in your dialoguing, perhaps?

CARMELA: Excuse me?

DR. MELFI: I don't know you that well . . . we're trying to get to the root causes.

TONY: Like maybe you do things that you know, have some effect on me.

CARMELA: Oh, really?

TONY: What? People affect each other in life . . .

CARMELA: Oh, I get it. Is this how it works? You can't get answers out of him you start looking for someone else to point a finger at?

TONY: She's not sayin' anything. Why are you gettin' so defensive?

CARMELA: You know what? Maybe you should explore your own behavior. Maybe you pass out because you're guilty over something. Maybe the fact that you stick your dick in anything with a pulse, have you thought of exploring that as a root cause?

TONY: Very nice. That's very nice.

CARMELA: Mhm.

TONY: I told you months ago I broke it off with that Russian person. Right?

CARMELA: It's incredible . . . it's like people who smoke their whole lives and then sue the cigarette companies when they get cancer.

TONY: You agreed to come here. Forget it, this is fuckin' ridiculous.

CARMELA: Right, just sit there. Silence, anger, then you pass out and you blame the rest of the fuckin' world.

TONY: Yeah, I love you, too.

DR. MELFI: You're both very angry.

TONY: You must've been at the top of your fuckin' class. [LATER, IN THE CAR] Oh, Jesus Christ . . . What? Great. And I'm the one who doesn't fuckin' communicate?

CARMELA: You want to know what's wrong? After nineteen years of marriage, I find it very sad that we have to pay a stranger to teach us how to interact.

(Season 3, Episode 5, "Another Toothpick")

CARMINE: [ON THE PHONE] It's me. What, are you still asleep?

TONY: No, I was . . . doing somethin'.

CARMINE: I took John to dinner last night. Ralph's got a big problem, kid.

TONY: I thought you squashed it.

CARMINE: I did. Problem is I don't know if John's hearin' me.

TONY: So what are you gonna do about it?

CARMINE: Me? Nothin'.

TONY: What does that mean?

CARMINE: I didn't say nothin'. We share the Esplanade, Tony. I don't want that apple cart upset.

TONY: Yeah, then somebody should do somethin' about it.

CARMINE: I appreciate your thoughts.

TONY: You sayin' what I think you're sayin'?

CARMINE: I didn't say nothin'. All right then, I'll talk to you.

(Season 4, Episode 4, "The Weight")

JOHNNY SACK: How's the mousse?

PAULIE: Fuckin' great. I tell ya, the shit ya miss when you're inside? There was a week where I woulda killed for some Good and Plenties.

JOHNNY SACK: Shoulda told me. I woulda sent ya some.

PAULIE: I know you would've. See that's the thing though. What I need's not your problem.

JOHNNY SACK: What do ya mean?

PAULIE: Fuckin' Tony. Four months I'm up there like the Man in the Iron Mask. Not one visit, not even a fuckin' phone call.

JOHNNY SACK: The guy didn't reach out at all?

PAULIE: John, when do I ever complain?

JOHNNY SACK: Paulie, look, the guy's a boss. You visit a guy in the can these days . . . you know the Feds. You give someone the time of day, it's a criminal conspiracy.

PAULIE: So he can't phone? You fuckin' did. Even before I left, he was treatin' me like the ugly girl at the dance. I'm suckin' wind, and he's rollin' in it with that fuckin' Christ-killer.

JOHNNY SACK: Hesh?

PAULIE: Fuckin' Zellman, fuckin' real estate scam.

JOHNNY SACK: The Frelinghuysen Avenue thing. We had some words. Tony made it right.

PAULIE: It's a different one now. I'm not sure what it is. All I know is fuckin' Ralphie's goin' around braggin' about how much they're makin'. Listen, John, I know we talk sometimes. I tell you my problems, you tell me yours. And I have the highest regards for Carmine.

JOHNNY SACK: He thinks the world of you, also.

PAULIE: Even still, this shit don't leave the table, right?

JOHNNY SACK: I'm hurt that you even have to ask.

(Season 4, Episode 7, "Watching Too Much Television")

TONY: I think I know what happened to Ralph and if I'm right . . . he ain't comin' back. It was New York.

VITO: Johnny Sack?

CARLO: What was it? The fat joke?

TONY: I'm sure that didn't help. Carmine. This HUD thing we're into, they wanted a piece of it. I think they confronted Ralph—things went sour.

ALBERT: What'd he say—John?

TONY: Wasn't what he said so much as what he didn't say.

PAULIE: We're talkin' about New York here.

(Season 4, Episode 10, "The Strong, Silent Type")

PAULIE: Tony's really hot that you didn't counter offer.

JOHNNY SACK: God forbid this gets really bad. There could be a change.

PAULIE: Tony?

JOHNNY SACK: Suffice to say, no matter what happens now, or in the future . . . Carmine won't forget you. And as far as us talkin' like this.

PAULIE: It's just because we're old friends. And I know I can blow off a little steam with ya.

JOHNNY SACK: Cheaper than a bartender.

PAULIE: I'm only tryin' to bring good relations between the families. As I always do, and always will. No matter what happens, or who's in charge. If it's me, God forbid . . . or whoever.

(Season 4, Episode 11, "Calling All Cars")

PAULIE: Carmine, hey, what are ya doin' here?

CARMINE: I'm a guest. My housekeeper's daughter.

PAULIE: Small world. The groom's dad, is my third cousin. Beautiful ceremony, huh? So, listen. About all this stuff that's goin' on . . . Tony and all.

CARMINE: What's your name again?

PAULIE: Paulie Gualtieri. Jersey?

CARMINE: Your father was run over by a trolley, right?

PAULIE: Johnny talked to you about me, right?

CARMINE: Johnny who? Sack? Talk to me about what?

(Season 4, Episode 12, "Eloise")

TONY: Well, here I am. What is it?

JOHNNY SACK: We go back a long way, Tony. We've come way too far to let it all go to shit.

TONY: With all due respect, uh, you wanna go down memory lane, put it in second gear, huh?

JOHNNY SACK: The Esplanade now. I wish for Carmine's own sake he'd ease off.

TONY: Why don't ya tell him that?

JOHNNY SACK: He's so easily upset these days. His teeth. I'll tell ya that restaurant thing didn't help.

TONY: He hurt my appraiser. What was I supposed to do? It's on page four of the Boss Manual, John. Jesus.

JOHNNY SACK: You're preachin' to the choir, Tony. I mean, you don't even wanna hear how many of his decisions end up lightening my pockets.

TONY: Why you tellin' me all this, John?

JOHNNY SACK: Because at heart I know you're a pragmatist. As I am. I'm tellin' ya now. Carmine won't bend.

TONY: And I just told you, I won't.

JOHNNY SACK: If Carmine's health were bad. If something were to happen to him—God forbid. All of this unpleasantness would just . . .

TONY: John, Carmine's fine.

JOHNNY SACK: Yes. He's very healthy. Thank God. Call me.

TONY: [TO HIMSELF] Holy shit.

(Season 4, Episode 12, "Eloise")

If a Country Is Governed Wisely

If a country is governed wisely,
Its inhabitants will be content.
Since they dearly love their homes,
They aren't interested in travel.
People enjoy their food,
Take pleasure in being with their families,
And even though the next country is so close
That people can hear roosters crowing
And its dogs barking,
They are content to die of old age
Without ever having gone to see it.

Tao Te Ching ☯ 80

CASHIER: Decaf Cappuccino Primo, non-fat Magnifico, double Espresso Regulare. [TO PUSSY] I'll take you over here, sir.

PUSSY: I think I'll have an Espresso. Paul, you want anything?

PAULIE: They got any, just coffee?

CASHIER: Our cafe du jour is New Zealand Peaberry.

PAULIE: Madonn' . . . Whatever.

CASHIER: That's $4.20, pick it up over there. One medium du jour, one single Espresso Regulare!

⊕　⊕　⊕　⊕　⊕

PAULIE: Fuckin' Italian people. How did we miss out on this?

PUSSY: What?

PAULIE: Fuckin' Espresso, Cappuccino. We invented this shit and all these other cocksuckers are getting rich off of it.

PUSSY: Yeah, isn't it amazing?

PAULIE: Yeah, it's not just the money. It's a pride thing. All our food, pizza, calzone, buffalo moozadell', olive oil. These fucks had nothin'. They ate pootsie before we gave 'em the gift of our cuisine. But this, this is the worst. This Espresso shit.

(Season 1, Episode 2, "46 Long")

TONY: [TO ARIEL] What, are you kiddin' me? You know, most guys I know would be happy to get rid of their wife.

SILVIO: I tried explainin' the realities here . . . this guy's as stubborn as a fuckin' mule . . . he says it's principle. I think we gotta . . . you know? That's why we called ya.

TONY: Look, I promised the father-in-law I wouldn't.

SILVIO: I didn't know what else to do!

TONY: You know, you're a stupid motherfucker.

ARIEL: I've heard it said. You kill me, and a dark cloud goes over Shlomo's house. Either way, there'll be no get unless restitution is made.

TONY: You really would let me kill you, wouldn't you? You stupid fuck.

ARIEL: You ever heard of the Masada? For two years . . . nine hundred Jews held their own against fifteen thousand Roman soldiers. They chose death before enslavement. And the Romans, where are they now?

TONY: You're lookin' at 'em, asshole.

(Season 1, Episode 3, "Denial, Anger, Acceptance")

MASSIVE: Mr. Herman Rabkin.

CHRISTOPHER: Hesh.

MASSIVE: I don't know him personally, but I know his history. In the late 50s and 60s, he owned F-Note Records.

CHRISTOPHER: I don't know what it was fuckin' called, but yeah, Hesh was in the music business.

MASSIVE: A little situation here. A distant but deceased quasi-cousin on my mother's side, Little Jimmy Willis, 50s legend. Two seminal hit records was his legacy. Drug tragedy. *Such A Fool* . . .

ADRIANA: Oh, I love that! They play it all the time on oldies radio!

MASSIVE: Ol' Herman? He's just another in a long line of white motherfuckers stealin' royalties from the black man that made him the money in the first place. Jimmy's mother out in San Bernadino, who I'm content to call my aunt, is owed that money.

CHRISTOPHER: Hesh is the world's sweetest guy. But I've heard his opinions on giving back pieces of Israel, I can only imagine what he's gonna say about this shit.

MASSIVE: Feel free to enjoy the food and any other enjoyments. [WALKS AWAY]

WAITER: Champagne, sir, ma'am?

[AFTER THE PARTY]

CHRISTOPHER: Yeah. That guy's a gangster? I'm a gangster! I'm an O.G., "Original Gangster," not him, fuckin' lawn jockey. But he's got the fly Hamptons house. Alec Baldwin comes over, Whitney Houston. What do I got? I sit in a fuckin' pork store, for Christ's sake. But the moolies, they got it goin' on. And they're on TV.

ADRIANA: And they don't take no shit!

CHRISTOPHER: Soprano crew, it's always secret this, omerta that. Fuckin' gets on my nerves. Junior with his moldy ol' sweaters, and he's a lousy fuckin' boss!

ADRIANA: And you were just feelin' so good about yourself!

CHRISTOPHER: Our thing once ruled the music business, did you know that?

ADRIANA: No.

CHRISTOPHER: We bankrolled acts, blacks, everybody. Paid the DJs or busted heads to get 'em played on the air.

ADRIANA: There were some great Italian singers.

CHRISTOPHER: Fuckin' A. Frankie Valli, Dion, The Rascals, the whole Philly thing. My dad used to talk about those guys. Now? Fuckin' drum machine, some ignorant poetry and any fuckin' fourth-grade dropout ditsoon is Chairman of the Board. Gangsta.

ADRIANA: [ABOUT THE RADIO] Talk about Paisan pride! Go, Jovi!

(Season 1, Episode 10, "A Hit Is a Hit")

MEADOW: I just don't think sex should be a punishable offense.

TONY: You know, honey, that's where I agree with you. I don't think sex should be a punishable offense either. But I *do* think that talkin' about sex at the breakfast table *is* a punishable offense, so no more sex talk, okay?

MEADOW: It's the 90s, parents are supposed to discuss sex with their children.

TONY: Yeah, but that's where you're wrong. Y'see, out there, it's the 1990s, but in this house, it's 1954.

(Season 1, Episode 11, "Nobody Knows Anything")

CARMELA: So, what did she have to say for herself?

TONY: The usual shit. Wasn't my fault.

CARMELA: There was designer drugs there, Tony. So what did you say?

TONY: I don't know, I yelled. What the fuck else am I gonna do?

CARMELA: There has to be consequences. What kind of parents would we be if we let her get away with this?

TONY: Typical?

CARMELA: Plenty of parents still crack the whip.

TONY: Yeah, that's what they tell ya.

CARMELA: I cannot wait until she goes off to college.

TONY: Oh, right, so you can be fucked up with the Empty Nest Syndrome and go on Wellbutrin like your sister.

CARMELA: As a parent today you are over a barrel no matter what you do. If you take away the car you become her chauffeur. You ground her, you gotta stay home weekends and be prison guard.

TONY: And if you throw her out the social services will bring her back and we'd be in front of the judge. She's not eighteen yet.

CARMELA: That's your solution, to throw your daughter out?

TONY: All I'm sayin', with the laws today, you can't even restrain your kid physically, 'cause she could sue you for child abuse.

CARMELA: There has to be consequences.

TONY: And there will be. Let's just not overplay our hand 'cause if she finds out we're powerless, we're fucked.

(Season 2, Episode 3, "Toodle-Fucking-Oo")

TONY: All right, what's goin' on with you?

ANTHONY JR.: Nothin'.

TONY: Nothin'. You know, that "No God," shit. That upset your mother very much.

ANTHONY JR.: It's not, "No God." It's just God is dead.

TONY: Who said that?

ANTHONY JR.: Nitch. He's a nineteenth-century philosopher from Germany. Anyway, that's why I'm not gettin' confirmed.

TONY: Enough with that shit, all right? Your confirmation's comin' up this weekend, and you are gettin' confirmed!

ANTHONY JR.: That sucks my nut!

TONY: Hey! You got a lot of balls, you know that? You go to Catholic school like your mother wants it!

ANTHONY JR.: Yeah, what does she know?

TONY: She knows that even if God is dead, you're still gonna kiss his ass.

(Season 2, Episode 7, "D-Girl")

TONY: I wanna spend more time with A.J.

CARMELA: It's the other one you should spend time with. She's almost out of the house.

TONY: Hey, I'm not worried about Meadow. Meadow could take care of herself.

CARMELA: Why the sudden burst of fatherhood?

TONY: Can you say anything without it bein' sarcastic?

CARMELA: You're right. I'm sorry. I think it's a good idea. He adores you. He never gets to spend enough time with you.

TONY: Yeah, well . . .

CARMELA: I was reading in *Time* the other day this study at Harvard. A father's support is absolutely linked to a boy's later capacity to manage frustrations . . . to explore new circumstances and to do well in school.

TONY: The kid needs to toughen up.

CARMELA: I'm not talking about toughening up, I'm talking about opening up.

TONY: Somebody needs to teach that kid some street smarts. Not to be a sucker. Not to be involved with the wrong people. I don't want another Christopher on my hands. I mean, look at him. He's lucky to be alive. [ABOUT JACKIE JR.] That other poor prick they found dead. The kid was twenty-three or somethin'.

(Season 2, Episode 10, "Bust Out")

CARMELA: [READING FROM *THE NEW YORK TIMES*] Italy was relieved today upon learning that the country's high court had ruled that influence-peddling is not a crime. Said Franco Ferroti, an Italian sociologist . . . "Essentially the judges are saying what everybody believes." He was referring to *raccomandazione*, the Italian custom of seeking special treatment from people in power. "This is our version of the Protestant ethic," Mr. Ferroti said. The case concerned the clerk of a civil court in Potenza who was jailed for promising to speed up someone's trial. Evidence showed that he received eighty-eight pounds of fish in return for his assistance.

(Season 4, Episode 1, "For All Debts Public and Private")

BACALA: [READING] In protest of Columbus' role in the genocide of America's native peoples, unquote. To launch their protest, the Native Americans and their sympathizers plan to begin a death watch tomorrow over the statue of Columbus in Christopher Columbus Park.

PATSY: Some fuckin' balls bad-mouthin' America, especially now.

FURIO: I thought that Columbus was the hero of America.

RALPH: Nah, see it's these Indians and the commie fucks. They wanna paint Columbus as a slave trader instead of an explorer.

CHRISTOPHER: Well ya gotta admit they did get massacred, the Indians.

SILVIO: It's not like we didn't give 'em a buncha shit to make up for that. Land. Reservations. And now they got the casinos.

VITO: What the fuck we ever get we didn't have to work our balls off for?

BACALA: I wouldn't mind sittin' on my ass all day, smokin' mushrooms and collectin' government checks.

SILVIO: You know what it is? I'll tell ya what it is. Anti-Italian discrimination. Columbus Day is a day of Italian pride. It's our holiday and they wanna take it away.

FURIO: Fuck them. But I never liked Columbus.

THE GUYS: Oh! Hey!

EUGENE: Why?

FURIO: In Napoli, a lotta people are not so happy for Columbus, 'cause he was from Genoa.

RALPH: What's the problem with Genoa?

FURIO: The North of Italy always have the money and the power. They punish the South since hundreds of years. Even today, they put up their nose at us like we're peasants. [SPITS] I hate the North.

VITO: Jesus, take it easy.

(Season 4, Episode 3, "Christopher")

CONCETTA LONGO-MURPHY: Looking out at this audience of proud, strong, beautiful women, how far we have come in this American journey. Look how we've both preserved the tradition of our ancestors and managed to become new Italian-American women. Such flair we have added to our image. And yet America still sees us as pizza makers and Mama Leone's. Well, it is your job, ladies, to spread the word. Our grandmothers may have been dressed in black, but we're in Moschino and Armani. For those who say Italian-Americans eat smelly cheese and sip cold wine, tell them we're from the land of aromatic Asiago and supple Barolo. If they say spaghetti and meatballs, you tell them orchiette with broccoli rabe. If they say John Gotti, you tell them Rudolph Giuliani. A Princeton study showed that seventy-four percent of Americans associated Italian-Americans with organized crime. Why would they do this? Because of the way the media depicts us. Again . . . it is our job to make sure people know the other side of Italian-American culture. The educated, wage-earning, law-abiding side. Because isn't that who we truly are? Thank you.

(Season 4, Episode 3, "Christopher")

CARMELA: [EXPLAINING TO TONY ABOUT ANTHONY JR.] His history teacher, Mr. Cushman, is teaching your son that if Columbus was alive today, he would go on trial for crimes against humanity like Milosevic in, you know, Europe.

TONY: Your teacher said that?

ANTHONY JR.: It's not just my teacher, it's the truth. It's in my history book.

TONY: So you finally read a book and it's bullshit.

CARMELA: Tony.

TONY: Look, ya had to walk in Columbus' shoes and see what he went through. People thought the world was flat, for cryin' out loud. Then he lived on an island with a bunch a naked savages on it, I mean, that took a lotta guts. You remember when we went to Florida—the heat? And those bugs?

ANTHONY JR.: Oh, like it took guts to murder people and put 'em in chains.

CARMELA: He was a victim of his time.

ANTHONY JR.: Who cares, it's what he did.

TONY: He discovered America is what he did. He was a brave Italian explorer. And in this house Christopher Columbus is a hero. End of story.

(Season 4, Episode 3, "Christopher")

SILVIO: [ABOUT REDCLAY] Maybe we oughta just whack this prick.

TONY: Who the fuck are you kiddin'? All you thought about was blackjack.

SILVIO: What?

TONY: You think this day in the country was free, don't you? Well it wasn't. Fuckin' Chief Smith wants Frankie Valli to come up there and play a week. That's what this whole fuckin' junket was about.

SILVIO: Frankie?

TONY: Yeah, that's right. That's why he buttonholed me, goddammit. There's bad blood with Frankie's manager so the Chief wants me to call him directly. As payback for him reachin' out to Redclay. Well you're gonna make the fuckin' call.

SILVIO: Well I ain't seen Frankie for years—

TONY: Tough shit! You're makin' the fuckin' call! You and this fuckin' parade already!

SILVIO: I don't know what you're so hot about. They discriminate against all Italians as a group, when they disallow Columbus Day.

TONY: Oh will you fuckin' stop? Group. Group. What the fuck happened to Gary Cooper, that's what I'd like to know.

SILVIO: He died. Oh you mean 'cause he fought the Sioux in all those westerns.

TONY: No, fuck that. Gary Cooper. Now there was an American. The strong, silent type. He did what he had to do. He faced down the Miller Gang when, when none a those other assholes in town would lift a finger to help him. And did he complain? Did he say, oh, I come from this poor Texas-Irish-illiterate-fuckin'-background or whatever the fuck so leave me the fuck out of it . . . because my people got fucked over!

SILVIO: T . . . not for nothin', but you're gettin' a little confused here. A, that was the movies . . .

TONY: Oh what the fuck difference does that make? Columbus was so long ago he might as well have been a fuckin' movie! Images you said.

SILVIO: The point is, Gary Cooper . . . the real Gary Cooper . . . Or anybody named Cooper never suffered like the Italians. The meddigan like him, eh, he fucked everybody else. Italians, the Polacks, the blacks . . .

TONY: All right even if he was a meddigan around nowadays he'd be a member of some victims group. The fundamentalist Christians, the abused cowboys, the gays, whatever the fuck!

CHRISTOPHER: He was gay, Gary Cooper?

TONY: No! Are you listenin' to me?

SILVIO: Hey. People suffered.

TONY: Did you? Except for maybe the Feds?

SILVIO: My grandparents got spit on 'cause they were from Calabria.

TONY: Let me ask you a question. All the good things you got in your life. Did they come to you 'cause you're Calabrese? I'll tell ya the answer. The answer is no. You got a smart kid at Lackawanna College. You got a wife . . . who's a piece of ass. Least she was when you married her. You own one of the most profitable topless bars in North Jersey. Now did you get all this shit 'cause you're Italian? No, you got it 'cause you're you. 'Cause you're smart. 'Cause you're whatever the fuck. Where the fuck is our self-esteem? I mean . . . that shit doesn't come from—from Columbus or the Godfather or Chef-fuckin'-Boyar-Dee.

SILVIO: We gotta tiptoe around the Indians though, don't we? We can't call our teams the Braves or the Tomahawks or the—

TONY: You take it up with Frankie Valli when you talk to him.

(Season 4, Episode 3, "Christopher")

TONY: See that church? Your great grandfather helped build that almost eighty years ago. He was a stone mason, the old man. Came over from Avellino with four dollars in his pocket.

ANTHONY JR.: Yeah, but I saw in a book where you could get a hotel room for like ten cents a week then. Room service must have been like one or two cents a meal.

TONY: Room service? We're talkin' about history here, A.J. Your family's history. Newark's history.

ANTHONY JR.: Well who gives a shit about Newark?

TONY: I'm makin' a point. This neighborhood used to be beautiful. A hundred percent Italian. The 1920s, most of them right off the boat. Most Italians couldn't even find a church that wanted 'em. So what did they do, did they cry? Did they go to the government with their hand out? No. They took care of their own problems. They said you don't want us in your church? Fine. We'll build our own. A better one. I mean, look around, look at all these buildin's around here. Most of them are fallin' down to the ground. But that church is still standin'. You know why?

ANTHONY JR.: The bricks?

TONY: 'Cause our people give a shit, that's why. Every Sunday Italians from the old neighborhood, they drive miles to come here to pray. They keep this place alive.

ANTHONY JR.: And so how come we never do?

TONY: Buy land, A.J., 'cause God ain't makin' any more of it. Hey, this is advice I'm impartin' to you as your father.

(Season 4, Episode 7, "Watching Too Much Television")

TONY: Well I analyzed it. There's two endings for a guy like me. High-profile guy. Dead . . . or in the can. Big percent of the time.

DR. MELFI: You've never talked this frankly.

TONY: Even with all this terrorism shit, the government has resources up the ass. As far as legal bills are con—

DR. MELFI: Anthony.

TONY: What?

DR. MELFI: Why don't you give it up?

TONY: Oh. You didn't let me finish. There's a third way . . . To wrap it up. You rely only on family.

DR. MELFI: Not many men could survive without the love and support of their wife and children—

TONY: No-no-no-no-no, I'm talkin' about business. You trust only blood. A friend of mine . . . A guy whose name you would know. Stayed out of the can and in charge, livin' in Florida 'til he was eighty-one years old . . . 'Cause he only gave orders to his son. No other conversations that could come back in testimony.

DR. MELFI: His son?

TONY: No, not A.J. What I've been dealt is my nephew. He's got his act together, that kid. And over the last coupla months I started the process of bonding him to me inseparably.

DR. MELFI: How?

TONY: Well that we can't get into.

DR. MELFI: Didn't your uncle do that with you? You said his life is like a desert.

TONY: I'm forty-two, I'm already more successful than my uncle ever was. You seen my house.

(Season 4, Episode 1, "For All Debts Public and Private")

Fill Your House with Gold and Jade

Fill your house with gold and jade
And it can no longer be guarded.

Tao Te Ching ☯ 9

CARMELA: [ABOUT THE FBI] Think they're gonna come over the weekend?

TONY: They're comin' someday. Where's the rest of the money?

CARMELA: It's everywhere.

TONY: Well, get it. What else?

CARMELA: How 'bout your phone numbers?

TONY: Anybody who's anybody's in my head. What's the matter?

CARMELA: Nothin', just here we go. Here. [TONY HANDS HER THE GUNS]

TONY: Why now? Why the fuck now, just when things were goin' good?

⊕   ⊕   ⊕   ⊕   ⊕

[UPSTAIRS]

MEADOW: Boot your computer, the cops are comin'!

ANTHONY JR.: So?

MEADOW: You want them to see all that porno you downloaded?

ANTHONY JR.: Shit!

⊕   ⊕   ⊕   ⊕   ⊕

TONY: All right, you better give me your jewelry.

CARMELA: Oh, Jesus!

TONY: Hey, they know we can't produce receipts, you want them stealin' this shit from us? [ABOUT CARMELA'S ENGAGEMENT RING] Come on.

CARMELA: I'm not giving you my engagement ring, this isn't stolen. Is it?

TONY: No. What do you think I am?!

(Season 1, Episode 8, "The Legend of Tennessee Moltisanti")

[THE FBI WATCHING A SURVEILLANCE CAMERA OF THE SOPRANOS' BASEMENT]

GRASSO: Hey. He's got the Black & Decker. I got one of those.

HARRIS: Hundred and twenty gallon water heater.

CUBITOSO: My house we're shivering after a shower and a half.

HARRIS: Whoa, wait a minute.

S.E.T. 1: What?

HARRIS: [TO S.E.T. 1] Go back. Look at the brown water. Right there, freeze it.

CUBITOSO: What, Ike?

HARRIS: You don't see it? Creep forward . . . give us some magni-fication.

CUBITOSO: That baby's gonna blow.

LIPARI: My dad was a plumber. Tony got about six months left to go on that lining.

GRASSO: Aw. It's a shame that we can't warn him.

HARRIS: Maybe during the discovery phase of his RICO trial we can inform his lawyer that Tony needs a plumber.

(Season 3, Episode 1, "Mr. Ruggerio's Neighborhood")

TONY: I work hard all day to pay for this . . . six thousand square foot house, big screen TVs, food on the table, video games, all kinds of scooters and bicycles, Columbia University . . . and for what? To come home to this?!

ANTHONY JR.: Sucks to be you.

(Season 3, Episode 13, "The Army of One")

ADRIANA: Holy shit. Oh my God. These diamonds . . .

CHRISTOPHER: Harry Winston, baby. It's got more carats than Bugs Bunny.

(Season 4, Episode 2, "No-Show")

CARMELA: So you've had a one-legged one now, huh? That's nice. You've had quite a time on my watch . . . the pre-school assistant, the weightlifter . . .

TONY: Least I never stole from you.

CARMELA: Who stole, Tony? Who? Me?

TONY: My own wife. Forty grand. From the birdfeeder.

CARMELA: The birdfeeder? Listen to yourself. You sound demented.

(Season 4, Episode 13, "Whitecaps")

Only One in Ten

Between their births and their deaths,
Three out of ten are attached to life,
Three out of ten are attached to death,
Three out of ten are just idly passing through.
Only one knows how to die and stay dead
And still go on living.

Tao Te Ching ☯ 50

CHRISTOPHER: I'm goin' to hell, T.

TONY: You're not goin' anywhere's but home.

CHRISTOPHER: I crossed over to the other side.

TONY: You what?

CHRISTOPHER: I saw a tunnel, and a white light. I saw my father in hell.

PAULIE: Get the fuck outta here.

CHRISTOPHER: And the bouncer said that I'd be there too when my time comes.

PAULIE: What bouncer?

CHRISTOPHER: The Emerald Piper. That's our hell. It's an Irish Bar where it's St. Patrick's Day everyday forever. Mikey Palmice and Brendan Filone were there, too. They were friends.

PAULIE: Those two guys hated each other.

TONY: Christopher, you gotta relax. Okay? You just need some rest.

CHRISTOPHER: They're friends now. They were playin' dice with two Roman soldiers and a bunch of the Irish guys.

PAULIE: It doesn't make sense.

CHRISTOPHER: And the Irish, they were winnin' every roll. And then Mikey gave me a message for both of you.

TONY: A message.

CHRISTOPHER: Yeah. Yeah, he said tell Tony and Paulie, three o'clock.

PAULIE: Three o'clock?

CHRISTOPHER: This fuckin' morphine drip, I don't think it's workin'. I don't feel a fuckin' thing.

TONY: You gotta be careful with that.

PAULIE: That was all he said?

CHRISTOPHER: Who?

PAULIE: Mikey. Three o'clock?

CHRISTOPHER: Yeah.

PAULIE: What was he wearin'?

TONY: Come on, let's go. He needs his rest.

CHRISTOPHER: He had on a gangster suit . . . pinstripe. Old-fashioned style.

TONY: Hey . . . that was a dream. Forget about it. Okay? I'm gonna take you home soon.

PAULIE: Do they know that this kid likes his chemistry set a little too much?

⊕   ⊕   ⊕   ⊕   ⊕

CHRISTOPHER: Fuck!

PAULIE: Just tryin' to tidy up the place. Go back to sleep.

CHRISTOPHER: Tidying up?

PAULIE: How you doin'?

CHRISTOPHER: I'm doin'.

PAULIE: I'll tell ya, I'm still baffled by this three o'clock thing, though.

CHRISTOPHER: I wish I had more for ya, Paulie. But that's all he said.

PAULIE: Let me ask you a question.

CHRISTOPHER: Yeah?

PAULIE: That bouncer that sent you back, did he have horns on his head?

CHRISTOPHER: No. He was just some big Irish goon in old-fashioned clothes.

PAULIE: Did anybody there have horns? Or buds for horns? Those goat bumps?

CHRISTOPHER: Paulie, it was fuckin' hell, okay? My father said he loses every hand of cards he plays. And every night at midnight, they whack him the same way he was whacked in life and it's painful. Night after night. Does that sound like fuckin' heaven to you?

PAULIE: Was it hot?

CHRISTOPHER: Yeah. I don't know. What the fuck?

PAULIE: The heat woulda been the first thing you noticed. Hell is hot. That's never been disputed by anybody. You didn't go to hell! You went to Purgatory, my friend.

CHRISTOPHER: I forgot all about Purgatory.

PAULIE: Purgatory. A little detour on the way to Paradise.

CHRISTOPHER: How long you think we gotta stay there?

PAULIE: Now that's different for everybody. You add up all your mortal sins and multiply that number by fifty. Then you add up all your venial sins and multiply that by twenty-five. You add 'em together, and that's your sentence. I figure I'm gonna have to do about six thousand years before I get accepted into Heaven. And six thousand years is nothin' in Eternity terms. I can do that standin' on my head. It's like a coupla days here.

(Season 2, Episode 9, "From Where to Eternity")

TONY: Christopher was clinically dead . . . for about a minute. He thinks he had one of those near death experiences. Says he visited hell and they told him he'd be back permanent.

DR. MELFI: Who's "they"?

TONY: It's bullshit. It was a dream combined with the morphine. But now he thinks he's gonna go to hell when he dies. He's all fucked up over it.

DR. MELFI: Do you think he'll go to hell?

TONY: No. He's not the type that deserves hell.

DR. MELFI: Who do you think does?

TONY: The worst people. The twisted and demented psychos who kill people for pleasure. The cannibals, the degenerate bastards that molest and torture little kids and they kill babies. The Hitlers, the Paul Pots. Those are the evil fucks that deserve to die. Not my nephew.

DR. MELFI: What about you?

TONY: What? Hell? You been listenin' to me? No. For the same reasons. We're soldiers. You know, soldiers don't go to hell. It's war. Soldiers, they kill other soldiers. We're in a situation where everybody involved knows the stakes, and if you're gonna accept those stakes . . . you gotta do certain things. It's business. We're soldiers. We follow codes. Orders.

DR. MELFI: So does that justify everything that you do?

TONY: Excuse me, let me tell you somethin'. When America opened the flood gates, and let all us Italians in . . . what do you think they were doin' it for? Because they were tryin' to save us from poverty? No, they did it because they needed us. They needed us to build their cities and dig their subways and to make 'em richer. The Carnegies, and the Rockefellers, they needed worker bees and there we were. But some of us didn't want to swarm around their hive and lose who we were. We wanted to stay Italian and preserve the things that meant somethin' to us. Honor, and family and loyalty. And some of us wanted a piece of the action. Now, we weren't educated like the Americans. But we had the balls to take what we wanted. And those other fucks, those other, the G.P. Morgans, they were crooks and killers, too. But that was their business, right? The American Way.

(Season 2, Episode 9, "From Where to Eternity")

The Best Way of Employing a Man

The best way of employing a man
Is to serve under him.

Tao Te Ching ☯ 68

HERMAN: So your uncle resents that you're the boss.

SILVIO: Sadness accrues.

HERMAN: Your uncle's had a hard-on his whole life. First against your father, his younger brother, 'cause he was a made man before him. And now, *you*. So sure he can't stomach your telling him what to do.

TONY: Hesh . . . I love the man.

HERMAN: The man is driven in toto by his insecurities.

(Season 1, Episode 1, "Pilot")

TONY: So one of us captains gotta step up. Lack of control at the top is fuckin' up this whole family.

RAYMOND: Well, that's true.

LARRY BOY: You can say that again.

TONY: I know if the old man were here instead of in that cell in Spring-field, he'd say, "Raymond, this is your moment."

RAYMOND: Go easy with the grease gun, okay?

TONY: What?

RAYMOND: Well, you're the Boy Wonder, both him and Jackie both had you picked from day one.

TONY: Hey, you got the age, you got the seniority.

RAYMOND: I also got an eighteen-year-old with MS, okay? I told Nucci I'd be doin' less, not more.

TONY: With all due respect to your crippled kid, you just don't want a wire up your ass. You don't want the headache.

RAYMOND: You see, that's why you should be the boss, you're so fucking smart. And, it's physically challenged.

LARRY BOY: Why don't we run this thing like a council?

JIMMY: Larry, the old guy set this up as a paramilitary organization. We need a supreme commander at the top, not the fuckin' Dave Clark Five.

RAYMOND: Face it T . . . you and Junior are gonna have to duke it out. You've gotta be boss.

TONY: Number one, I'm not the man. Number two, he's got New York behind him.

LARRY BOY: If anything, God bless your uncle. But he's livin' in the wrong century. And New York knows it.

JIMMY: You want it, T. You'll get their okay.

RAYMOND: It's the right thing. It's inevitable.

TONY: I don't want no disturbance.

(Season 1, Episode 4, "Meadowlands")

TONY: My uncle, he's got me in a box, where I gotta do something I don't wanna do. Then there's my mother. I pay four grand a month for this place and she acts like I'm an Eskimo, pushin' her out to sea.

DR. MELFI: She's testing. Same as your uncle.

TONY: Like little kids.

DR. MELFI: There's a good book about this. I'll give you the name.

TONY: No, I read, I go right out.

DR. MELFI: It's strategies . . . for coping with elder family.

TONY: Can't fuckin' spank 'em!.

DR. MELFI: Would it hurt you to let your mother *think* that she's still in charge? You have children, you know what they're like. You know that sometimes it's important to let them *have the illusion of being in control.*

(Season 1, Episode 4, "Meadowlands")

TONY: Uncle Junior . . . I need to talk to you. I came in heavy, like you said, but I don't wanna use it. Our friend Jackie has died.

JUNIOR: I heard.

TONY: And we need a leader.

JUNIOR: We do.

TONY: And I don't want any confusion or misunderstanding.

JUNIOR: Yes.

TONY: Sopranos have been waiting a long time to take the reins. That's why I want it to be you, Uncle Jun.

JUNIOR: This is your decision?

TONY: It is.

JUNIOR: You speak for the captains?

TONY: I can.

JUNIOR: Come here. You crazy chadrool. You had me worried there.

TONY: What do you think, I'm gonna mess with a guy like you? Huh? What, you been pumpin' iron? Look at you, strong as a bull. Hey, call Parcells, give this guy a tryout, huh? Come here. [THEY EMBRACE]

JUNIOR: Tony . . . the bullshitter.

TONY: Just one thing, one thing.

JUNIOR: What is it?

TONY: You know I can't be perceived to lose face, right? So . . . Bloomfield, and the Paving Union. It's my asking price. [JUNIOR NODS AGREEMENT] Congratulations.

(Season 1, Episode 4, "Meadowlands")

SILVIO: Tell me why this was a smart move, to make Junior the Big Willie.

TONY: Look at him, he's content. Thinks he's the king of kings. Truth is, every decision is made by me.

JIMMY: I still worry about the money end.

TONY: That's 'cause that's what you do, you worry. He doesn't know what we kick back to Jackie. We're gonna do good. The point is, he's got the title. He's a happy fuckin' camper. The house is secure.

SILVIO: Yeah, only now we got a brand-new lightning rod on top to take the hits.

HESH: Smart. Very smart.

LARRY BOY: Yeah, and now you got Bloomfield and the union chair.

TONY: Well, otherwise, you'd fuck me, Larry, but you wouldn't respect me in the morning, would you?

JIMMY: As long as you guarantee to keep the old fart in line.

TONY: Hey, I still love that man. I'm his favorite nephew. Look at him, over there with my ma. Those people went through World War II.

(Season 1, Episode 4, "Meadowlands")

TONY: Bobby Baccilieri, the last man standin'.

BACALA: I don't wanna say nothin', Tony.

PUSSY: You don't wanna get yourself in trouble.

TONY: A lot of funerals in your corner of the world, huh, Bobby? Fuckin' boosta, what'd you have to do, refinance your house? Don't look at the floor, Bobby, look at me. I want you to talk to that bald cocksucker who calls himself my father's brother. Tell him we're gonna let him keep on earnin'. Subsistence level. He'll be able to pay his defense lawyers.

BACALA: Already, let me say it for him, thank you.

TONY: Now, Bobby, you're gonna hear some high-end shit. And A, I hope you can understand it and B, I hope you keep it between this room and Junior. Because if you don't, I promise you, they're gonna find pieces of you in eight different dumpsters

BACALA: I inherited Junior. I don't think you got reason to talk to me this way. I always liked you.

TONY: Bullshit. But we'll assume you do now. You tell my uncle that he gets to keep five percent, five percent of his shy, his sports bettin', same with the coke. The Joint Fitters Union is all his, okay? Now, Bobby, listen. This is very important. He also gets to keep his stripes. As far as the Feds are concerned they got the boss of the family in jail, awaitin' trial. And if they hear different it creates confusion. Now, as far as the rest of everything that Junior owns . . . it's now mine.

(Season 2, Episode 2, "Do Not Resuscitate")

Do You Have the Patience to Wait?

The ancient Masters were profound and subtle.
Their wisdom was unfathomable.
There is no way to describe it;
All we can describe is their appearance.
They were careful
As someone crossing an iced-over stream.
Alert as a warrior in enemy country.
Clear as a glass of water.
Do you have the patience to wait
Till your mud settles and the water is clear?

Tao Te Ching ☯ 15

CHRISTOPHER: You ever feel like nothin' good was ever gonna happen to you?

PAULIE: Yeah. And nothin' did. So what? I'm alive, I'm survivin'.

CHRISTOPHER: That's it. I don't wanna just survive. It says in these movie writing books that every character has an arc. You understand? Like everybody starts out somewheres and then they do something, or somethin' gets done to them, it changes their life. That's called their arc. Where's my arc? All right, take Richard Kimble, right? No, that's no good, his arc is run, run, jump off the dam . . . run . . . Keanu Reeves, *Devil's Advocate*. You see that?

PAULIE: Oh, right!

CHRISTOPHER: Keanu's a lawyer, gets all turned on by money, power, and the devil. Then his wife says to him, "You're not the man I married," leaves him. You see the arc? He starts down here, he ends up here. Where's my arc, Paulie?

PAULIE: Kid, Richard Kimble, the Devil's whatever, those are all make-believe. Hey, I got no arc, either. I was born, grew up, spent a few years in the Army, a few more in the can, and here I am. A half a wise guy. So what?

CHRISTOPHER: I got no identity. I mean, even Brendan Filone's got an identity, he's dead. I killed that fuckin' Emil Kolar and nothing. I don't even move up a notch. All I got is nightmares. That Polish, Czech, Slavic, whatever the fuck he is, is hauntin' me in my dreams every night.

⊕   ⊕   ⊕   ⊕   ⊕

PUSSY: That happens. The more of them you do, the better you'll sleep. I had one prick chasin' me for months in my dreams.

CHRISTOPHER: I feel like he's tryin' to tell me somethin'. That we fucked up the night that we buried him.

PUSSY: We didn't fuck up.

CHRISTOPHER: And I'm in danger.

PUSSY: Could I ask you a question? Why the fuck would he want to tell you you're in danger considering you put a fuckin' moon roof in the back of his head?

CHRISTOPHER: What did we do wrong that night? The gun was hot, so the slugs in his head couldn't be traced back to me.

PUSSY: You know who had an arc? Noah.

(Season 1, Episode 8, "The Legend of Tennessee Moltisanti")

TONY: It's good to be in somethin' from the ground floor. And I came too late for that, I know. But lately, I'm gettin' the feelin' that I came in at the end. The best is over.

DR. MELFI: Many Americans, I think, feel that way.

TONY: I think about my father. He never reached the heights like me. But in a lot of ways he had it better. He had his people, they had their standards, they had pride. Today, what do we got?

(Season 1, Episode 1, "Pilot")

TONY: Richie, you know I love ya. You're like my big brother, okay? You're gonna be taken care of. What was yours before you went away will be yours again. You just gotta give us some time.

RICHIE: Jeez, Anthony, you'll do that for me?

TONY: Hey, fuck you.

RICHIE: What's mine is not yours to give me.

(Season 2, Episode 3, "Toodle-Fucking-Oo")

TONY: Yeah?

DR. MELFI: It's Dr. Melfi.

TONY: Yeah, so?

DR. MELFI: I tried your other number. If you want, I could fit you in tomorrow at two thirty. So, do I put you down?

TONY: Nah, fuck it.

DR. MELFI: Why do you say that?

TONY: Gettin' by without it. There's no cure for life.

(Season 2, Episode 5, "Big Girls Don't Cry")

PUSSY: Anthony.

ANTHONY JR.: Go away.

PUSSY: No. I'm your sponsor. We need to talk. You need to listen. You know, you see your parents as these great big dictators. These disciplinarians. But I know your Dad from the time he was younger than you.

ANTHONY JR.: Yeah, what difference does it make?

PUSSY: Listen to me, all right? You listenin'?

ANTHONY JR.: Yeah.

PUSSY: I know him. I was sixteen years old and my kid sister, Nucci, she had the spinal meningitis and she got to a point where she couldn't breathe.

ANTHONY JR.: She was real sick?

PUSSY: Yeah. And she was in the hospital, and your father, he was the only one, he came with me every day . . . He sat by her bed. He looked at her drawings. He watched her for me when I had to use the john or get somethin' to eat and . . . I was down there waitin' in line for a hamburger when she passed away.

ANTHONY JR.: She died, huh?

PUSSY: Yeah.

ANTHONY JR.: See, you know what really pisses me off about my dad? He did all these great things, then. Before he was my Dad. Now he's just an asshole.

(Season 2, Episode 7, "D-Girl")

CHRISTOPHER: All right. That's bent enough. Get the crow bar, pop the plate.

MATT: Sean, without fail, every time we're on a fuckin' job . . .

CHRISTOPHER: The adrenaline affects everybody differently. Big Pussy Bonpensiero, he started out as a cat burglar. One time he left a load so big, cop thought a bear was in the place.

SEAN: Pussy Bonpensiero started off chippin' safes like this?

CHRISTOPHER: Until he stepped up for Johnny Soprano during the unrest of '83.

SEAN: Back then when you did somethin', you got recognized.

CHRISTOPHER: When your time comes you either step up or you start lookin' for a new career.

(Season 2, Episode 8, "Full Leather Jacket")

TONY: Where's Carmine at?

JOHNNY SACK: No change whatsoever.

TONY: Where you at?

JOHNNY SACK: I think a movement from below is not palatable to the other bosses. It's what they fear most. A movement from outside, it's more forgivable. And more understandable, given the facts. I mean, you've been reasonable.

TONY: If I do it, what do you do for me?

JOHNNY SACK: I take a sad song and make it better. With the other families, as regards you. You're smart to have reservations. But there's differences between this and Castellano. Yes, you still got the four other families who could raise a stink. But Andy's my brother-in-law. I have their ear.

TONY: I'm gonna pass.

JOHNNY SACK: Fuck you talking about?

TONY: I'm taking all the risk.

JOHNNY SACK: Fuck were you talking about last time then? What would it take?

TONY: Fuck even one percentage point. All claims to my HUD business are irrogated.

JOHNNY SACK: All right.

TONY: Not yet. All future construction projects, sixty/forty in my favor.

(Season 4, Episode 13, "Whitecaps")

JOHNNY SACK: I was wondering . . . why the delay?

TONY: I was gonna call ya. You're not gonna be happy. I'm out. Whackin' a boss is bad for business. And now that he's settled?

JOHNNY SACK: We can weather it.

TONY: It's not just the internal upheaval. Mr. and Mrs. John Q. America, by and large they sit still for our shit. So people get ripped off? They figure it's not them. But if it's the fuckin' O.K. Corral out there? The Feds take heat . . .

JOHNNY SACK: Whew, Tony . . . this, this is very disappointing.

TONY: I know. But he's an old man. Come on, you're gonna get your chance soon enough.

JOHNNY SACK: Don't go into coaching, Tony. It's not your strong suit.

TONY: What I was gonna say . . .

JOHNNY SACK: Tomorrow I go into work . . . Creeps on this petty pace

. . . and I take orders from him again? Or that disgustin' fuckin' cocksucker idiot son of his?!

TONY: I shouldn't be hearing that.

JOHNNY SACK: Oh, really?

TONY: What I was gonna say was . . . it's a major step. But if you wanna do it, without me as a partner . . . you do what you gotta do. I will never, ever reveal any conversation we ever had.

JOHNNY SACK: The thing is we had those conversations. Your mouth was moving along with mine. So now we just go back about our business at the Esplanade like it never happened?

TONY: Well, yeah, that would be the healthy choice.

JOHNNY SACK: Healthy for who? Why the fuck would I ever trust somebody who would leave me holding my cock like this?

TONY: I shouldn't have heard that either.

JOHNNY SACK: Well . . . there you go. There's the fucking problem.

TONY: John, I still consider you a dear, dear friend.

(Season 4, Episode 13, "Whitecaps")

Act without Doing

Act without doing,
Work without effort.

Tao Te Ching ☯ **63**

JUNIOR: I'm sick and tired of sittin' around on my hands. I'm gonna get the hell out of here.

MELVOIN: Down to Boca with your lady friend?

JUNIOR: What the fuck you know about her?

MELVOIN: Works for the Joint Fitters Union, didn't somebody say? Runs their . . . labor management fund outside the Fed's oversight.

JUNIOR: If you can't get your friends jobs, what's the purpose of attaining success?

(Season 1, Episode 9, "Boca")

BOBBI: Ah! Ooh hoo. Mr. Soprano.

JUNIOR: Miss Sanfillipo.

BOBBI: I have a check here for you to sign.

JUNIOR: Twenty grand.

BOBBI: For research and development into furthering the art and science of metal and ceramic joint fittings.

JUNIOR: Where's our research and development take us this time?

BOBBI: I was thinking Boca Raton.

JUNIOR: My, my, you read my mind.

BOBBI: I'm all packed, baby.

(Season 1, Episode 9, "Boca")

SILVIO: So, Pasqualin'. I understand we got some business to discuss. The floor is yours.

PATSY: Go on, tell 'em.

LITTLE PAULIE: I drove out to Youngstown to see Uncle Paulie . . . and he was, I don't know . . . hopin' you could settle this shit with Ralph and the no-show carpenter jobs.

SILVIO: Ralph?

RALPH: Okay, for the record, I had my guy go over the books. We can do maybe two carpenter jobs, one no-show, one no-work.

PATSY: Two jobs. On a three hundred million dollar project?

SILVIO: Come on, Ralph. What's the real number?

RALPH: What, am I speakin' in tongues here? Two. Maybe I can do three.

LITTLE PAULIE: My uncle's lookin' for at least ten.

PATSY: I'm talkin' here. The guy's in the can. You think you wanna keep him happy maybe?

SILVIO: All right. Here it is. And this comes from [POINTS UP] For the duration, you will give Paulie five carpenter jobs. Two no-shows and three no-works. One of the no-shows our friend in Youngstown keeps. And one he gives to Chrissy here. The others, the no-work jobs, that's for Paulie. How he wants to distribute them.

RALPH: It is so decreed.

(Season 4, Episode 2, "No-Show")

LITTLE PAULIE: Hey, what are you doin'?

CHRISTOPHER: Breakin' my balls. What's it look like? I tell ya, this no-show shit is tough. Decidin' what not to wear to work. What not to put in my lunchbox.

PATSY: You're breakin' my heart. You should try sittin' here ten-thirty to three.

(Season 4, Episode 2, "No-Show")

JANICE: Don't you knock?

TONY: Listen, Jan, can we uh, shut this off a minute? I got somethin' I gotta ask ya.

JANICE: Sure.

TONY: It's a little awkward. It's about Ralph.

JANICE: That scumbag?

TONY: Yeah, well. I'm tryin' to find out about his sex life. Who would know better?

JANICE: He would. Ask him.

TONY: I can't. I can only ask you. I mean, is he weird about sex?

JANICE: Why are you interested in this?

TONY: I got my reasons. Managerial. You know, like the Army, it's got policies about this shit on account of combat.

JANICE: I have to tell you, Tony. I'm finding this entire conversation insulting.

TONY: Here we go.

JANICE: You're asking me to betray confidences. I mean, no matter what either one of us think of the guy . . .

TONY: Mm.

JANICE: Three thousand dollars.

TONY: How'd you come up with that figure?

JANICE: It's a number that I thought you'd say yes to.

TONY: You thought right.

(Season 4, Episode 8, "Mergers and Acquisitions")

The Highest Type of Ruler

The highest type of ruler is one of whose existence
The people are barely aware.
Next comes the one whom they love and praise.
Next comes the one whom they fear.

Tao Te Ching ☯ 17

TONY: I gotta be honest with you. I'm not gettin' any satisfaction from my work, either.

DR. MELFI: Why?

TONY: Well, because of RICO.

DR. MELFI: Is he your brother?

TONY: No. The RICO statutes. You know?

DR. MELFI: Oh, of course, right.

TONY: You read the papers? You know, the government's usin' electronic surveillance and various legal strategies to squeeze my business.

DR. MELFI: Do you have any qualms about how you actually . . . make a living?

TONY: Yeah. I find I have to be the sad clown. Laughin' on the outside, cryin' on the inside.

(Season 1, Episode 1, "Pilot")

JUNIOR: So what is it you want to talk about?

TONY: Octavian. You know, Augustus.

JUNIOR: Are you fuckin' with me?

TONY: No. Octavian became Augustus . . . forget about that. Bottom line: Augustus was a Caesar. And everybody loved him, right? You know why?

JUNIOR: I don't know that I give a fuck.

TONY: Everybody loved him because he never ate alone. Capish? It was the longest time of peace in Rome's history. He was a fair leader and all his people loved him for that . . . All right, remember the story you told me about the father bull talkin' to the son? They're up on this hill, they're lookin' out at a bunch of cows. And the son goes to the father, "Dad, why don't we run down there and fuck one of these cows?" Now you remember what the father said? The father said, "Son, why don't we walk down there and fuck 'em all?"

JUNIOR: I told you that? Why don't we fuck 'em all. That's funny.

TONY: Yeah.

JUNIOR: Okay, I get your point.

(Season 1, Episode 6, "Pax Soprana")

TONY: You okay with this?

JUNIOR: Do I have a choice?

TONY: Yeah, you got a choice. You could continue to run the game.

JUNIOR: You know I'm under fuckin' house arrest, you cute fuck.

TONY: Well, then take the bite I give you and be happy. Either way, I'm having the executive game.

JUNIOR: You know, your father and me started that game over thirty years ago. We were talking one day about how the credit card companies, you know, they worked their angle. They didn't care what the fuck you bought as long as you didn't pay all at once. They juice you to death, then you thank them for letting you have a card. You'd rather be juiced than pay all at once. There's a certain kind of player. That's why we call it The Executive Game. My brother Johnny was one keen motherfucker.

(Season 2, Episode 6, "The Happy Wanderer")

JUNIOR: You're a good boy, Richie.

RICHIE: It's gonna be good.

JUNIOR: Go on home. We'll talk. [RICHIE LEAVES]

BACALA: Fuckin' guy's fearless for his size.

JUNIOR: That's nice. Then what? He fuckin' dies and I can't even wear his shoes.

BACALA: What the fuck you talkin' about?

JUNIOR: Fuckin' loser. He couldn't sell it.

BACALA: Richie?

JUNIOR: Pay attention. You just may learn somethin' here. Who am I best off with? We best off with? Old man Profaci knew how to split his enemies. He couldn't fuckin' sell it. He's not respected. But Tony with his impulsiveness and selfishness. He's locked up in that fuckin' head of his. I'm better off with Tony. Definitely. I wanna see Anthony at the doctor's office tomorrow. What are you lookin' at?

BACALA: I'm in awe of you.

(Season 2, Episode 12, "The Knight in White Satin Armor")

[GAMBLING AT MANCUSO'S & SONS]

RALPH: Hello, Anthony. Ya look good.

TONY: Wanna drink?

RALPH: Another time, Anthony.

TONY: Another time. [RALPH NODS TO PAULIE, THEN TURNS AND WALKS AWAY.]

PAULIE: Let's whack this cocksucker and be done with it.

TONY: I'm here to enjoy myself.

[LATER, AT NUOVO VESUVIO]

SILVIO: "Another time, Anthony"?

TONY: Cocksucker turns his back on the boss?

SILVIO: *That* I couldn't believe.

TONY: Lucky I didn't put one in his fuckin' head.

SILVIO: On that front don't be surprised if Paulie pops the question. Ralphie's star is risin'. All those unions. Paulie can't come near that kinda cash for us.

TONY: Ralphie's a good earner.

SILVIO: Guy like that . . . loose cannon. You'll be leavin' your house, he'll pull a Jack Ruby on ya.

TONY: Why did I have to punch this fuckin' asshole?

SILVIO: Frankly . . . I was a little surprised.

TONY: Are you gonna start on me now, huh? He disrespected the Bing.

SILVIO: So, he's barred from the place.

TONY: He bashed that poor girl's brains in.

SILVIO: I hear ya. I know. It was a tragedy. The fact is though, she was not related to you by blood or marriage. She was not your goomar. Ralphie's a made guy, Ton'. All things considered, he's got a legitimate beef. Make him disappear. Or make nice. You only got two choices. And I would suggest something in the way of an apology.

TONY: Absolutely fuckin' not.

SILVIO: Do somethin' public to show there's no bad blood. Give him . . . give him a piece of the casino.

TONY: We're partnered with New York on that. And I don't want him that close to Johnny Sack.

SILVIO: You could bump him up to captain. It's what he's been wantin', ya know.

TONY: Ralphie a fuckin' captain? Over my dead body.

[NEXT SCENE, AT DINER]

RALPH: See that shit before? The look on Tony's face when I turned down that drink. Buy me a drink? Fuck you. He knew it was wrong what he did.

VITO: He is the boss. He could do what he wants.

GENE: Boss or no, you don't raise your hand to another made guy. Joe Mo from Mulberry Street. Exact same situation. He smacked that guy from North Bergen around. Huge problem.

RALPH: Course. Rules are rules, otherwise what? Fuckin' anarchy.

GENE: At the very least, Tony owes you an apology.

RALPH: The money I put in his pocket from construction alone he should hit his knees, this prick. What? You think I'm afraid of that fat fuck? No offense. I could see if it was his daughter. Or a niece of his. But all this over some dead whore. He had to be fuckin' her.

VITO: No. He knew you were fuckin' her.

RALPH: That's why, that's how he is. Like a dog with two bones.

(Season 3, Episode 8, "He Is Risen")

TONY: It's three a.m. and bam. Come wide awake.

DR. MELFI: Something specific?

TONY: It's a management problem. It's a situation with an underling. Now it's partly my fault. But he never shoulda done what he did.

DR. MELFI: What was it? Could you . . . tell me that?

TONY: Caused . . . early retirement . . . for somebody else. Particulars aren't important. He fucked up. Now ordinarily I would just, you know, put him out to pasture. But he's a very valuable piece of man-power.

DR. MELFI: Is it complicated by a personal relationship?

TONY: Been readin' that book you told me about. *The Art of War* by Sun Tzu. Here's this guy, a Chinese general. Wrote this thing twenty-four hundred years ago. And most of it still applies today. Balk the enemy's power. Force him to reveal himself.

DR. MELFI: I have to ask. Are you in any sort of danger?

TONY: No, no. Can I go on? Now most of the guys that I know they read Prince Matchabelli. And I had Carmela go and get the Cliff Notes once, and it was okay. But this book is much better about strategy.

(Season 3, Episode 8, "He Is Risen")

TONY: Jackie Jr. call you?

RALPH: No, why?

TONY: He called me.

RALPH: Oh . . . I'm sorry . . .

TONY: Nah, don't apologize. Anyway, I told him to take it up with you.

RALPH: Ton', what do you want me to do? I mean, you're the boss of the fam . . .

TONY: We talked about this. You were gonna give him a pass. But he should know. You don't want to create confusion and insubordination. But more important than the particular decision is that it happen in a timely fashion. But, fuck . . . why am I tellin' you? You know all this. You're a captain. Chain of command is very important in our thing.

(Season 3, Episode 13, "The Army of One")

HAYDU: Listen to me. It's not too late to cut your losses. Unlock me, give me the weapons. I promise you I will do whatever is in my power to help you.

CHRISTOPHER: Maybe. Let's come back to that.

HAYDU: You're bein' set up! He's lying to you, whoever he is.

CHRISTOPHER: It wouldn't make any difference.

HAYDU: What do you mean it wouldn't make any difference?!

CHRISTOPHER: He wants you dead.

(Season 4, Episode 1, "For All Debts Public and Private")

SILVIO: So you got a minute?

CARMELA: Who's that?

TONY: Nobody, go back to sleep.

CARMELA: Oh, hey, Sil.

SILVIO: How you doin', hon? [CARMELA WALKS AWAY.] This floor tile shit . . . misunderstanding. Patsy . . . Christopher.

TONY: It's a huge job, Sil. A lotta money at stake. You of all people should know that.

SILVIO: What are you, mad at me now?

TONY: You know you're gettin' to be a very strange man in your old age, you know that?

SILVIO: Why? I'm just askin'. Is it a hangin' offense or not?

TONY: Did you deliberately disobey me?

SILVIO: Of course not.

TONY: 'Cause Patsy says you gave the okay. This is after Chrissy talked to him.

SILVIO: Timeline got fucked up.

TONY: We go back a long way, Sil.

SILVIO: Indeed we do.

TONY: If in any way you feel like . . . Chrissy usurped you or anything like that, and you're tryin' to read me . . . That's not how it is.

SILVIO: Fine. Whole thing . . . Misunderstanding.

TONY: Truckload of floor tiles. You should be lookin' at what, thirty grand?

SILVIO: Should be about two grand there. I'll have the rest for ya later.

TONY: I know you will.

(Season 4, Episode 2, "No-Show")

JOHNNY SACK: I want you to sanction a hit on Ralph Cifaretto.

CARMINE: What, are you fuckin' kidding me?

JOHNNY SACK: He violated my wife's honor.

CARMINE: Ralph slept with Ginny?

JOHNNY SACK: He insulted her. He made a very insensitive joke about her body to some friends of ours.

CARMINE: What did he say?

JOHNNY SACK: I have to repeat it? My word's not good enough?

CARMINE: Not if you want him clipped over it.

JOHNNY SACK: He said she was havin' a ninety pound mole removed from her ass. The implication was that her ass is so big, she could have a mole that size removed from it.

CARMINE: It's an off-color remark, it was highly inappropriate. You want, I'll demand he's taxed. But clip him?

JOHNNY SACK: Is it all just about money?

CARMINE: I'll crack him good. I'll ask for two hundred grand.

JOHNNY SACK: Two hundred grand for insulting my wife. What's next Carmine, he gets to fuck her for a million?

CARMINE: He wants to fuck her?

JOHNNY SACK: I'm making a point! I'm talkin' about my wife's honor here. My honor.

CARMINE: We depend on this guy, there are millions of dollars at stake. We can't afford it, John.

JOHNNY SACK: A roomful of guys making fun of my wife and you're not gonna let me deal with this?

CARMINE: Not that way. My answer's gotta be no.

(Season 4, Episode 4, "The Weight")

CARMINE: Junior, can we do this already?

JUNIOR: Yeah, right. Johnny and Ralph Cifaretto, right? Ralph insulted John's wife?

JOHNNY SACK: That's correct.

JUNIOR: Who's on the wire now?

JOHNNY SACK: It's John, Corrado.

JUNIOR: Oh. So what did Ralph do exactly?

JOHNNY SACK: He made a very hurtful remark, it's not worth re-peating.

CARMINE: It's not important. Let's just agree it was unkind.

SILVIO: Let's point out too that it's only been alleged something was said.

JOHNNY SACK: He allegedly said what he said to a group of people . . . friends of ours.

JUNIOR: If you weren't there, how do you know it's true?

JOHNNY SACK: I'm not at liberty to say.

TONY: With all due respect, this is bullshit. Someone in my family's talkin' out of school and you're "not at liberty" to say who? I should be makin' the beef here.

JUNIOR: My nephew's right.

CARMINE: Let's stick to the issue. A horrible insult was made against Ginny. End of fuckin' story.

JUNIOR: So what does he want done about it?

JOHNNY SACK: I want to avenge her honor, as is my right to do.

TONY: All right, fine. You tell me who told you about it, we'll bring him in here. He corroborates what you're sayin', I'll give you Ralph on a platter.

JOHNNY SACK: Is nothing sacred? I mean, this is my wife we're talking about here. If this were years ago, would I even have had to ask? I mean, what's happened to this thing? For God's sake, we bend more rules than the Catholic Church.

TONY: All right, look. Let's assume for the sake of argument Ralph said what you think he said. Is clippin' him gonna unring that bell?

CARMINE: Nobody's getting clipped.

JOHNNY SACK: I want satisfaction.

SILVIO: Will you accept an apology?

JOHNNY SACK: That ship has sailed.

CARMINE: You're being unreasonable, John.

JOHNNY SACK: Ralph Cifaretto's the only one who knows how to handle the Esplanade? Put Pontecorvo in there.

CARMINE: There are millions of dollars at stake.

JOHNNY SACK: Again with the money?

CARMINE: Yeah, again with the money. It's settled, John. So either name a price or get the fuck over it.

(Season 4, Episode 4, "The Weight")

You Fight a War by Exceptional Moves

You govern a kingdom by normal rules;
You fight a war by exceptional moves.

Tao Te Ching ☯ 57

ARIEL: Yeah, tho' I walk through the valley of the shadow of death, I fear no evil for thou art with me.

TONY: Yeah, hold that thought. [TONY LEAVES THE ROOM, MAKES A CALL ON HIS CELLPHONE.]

HESH: Yeah.

TONY: Hesh . . . I'm here with my nonshellfish-eatin' friend and I gotta tell ya somethin', I'm tapped out. This guy won't listen to reason.

HESH: Didn't I tell ya? Didn't I warn you to keep away from those fanatics?

TONY: He's leavin' me no options, this guy's willin' to go down with the ship like no man I've ever seen!

HESH: Well, here's a thought. Maybe he's willing to go to the world to come, but if he's stuck here on this earth, I know one thing that no man wants to go through life without.

TONY: What? Oh. That's fuckin' brilliant.

HESH: Make like a mohel? Finish his bris.

TONY: Yeah. [AGREES AS HE HANGS UP] Paulie! Get the bolt cutters from outta the truck! Ariel, we're goin' to Plan B.

(Season 1, Episode 3, "Denial, Anger, Acceptance")

NEWSCASTER: This afternoon in Montclair, Anthony Soprano, who allegedly holds the rank of captain, or higher, in the Northern New Jersey Mafia, was wounded in what the victim claims was an attempted carjack. But sources in the FBI say it was a gangland execution gone awry. Soprano escaped with minor wounds and was taken to an undisclosed area hospital. However, one of his assailants, William Johnson "Peffle" Clayborn, was fatally wounded in the attack. Continuing now with . . .

LIVIA: Is this true?

JUNIOR: Why, you think they made it up?

LIVIA: But, how, how could this happen?!

JUNIOR: I don't know, I feel like I'm floatin' in space. He's gonna look for who did this to him.

LIVIA: Anthony? Well, of course he is!

JUNIOR: Livia, you understand what's goin' on here?

LIVIA: My son got shot and he got away!

JUNIOR: What do we do now? What the hell do we do now, Livia?

LIVIA: We go see him.

JUNIOR: Tony?

LIVIA: Of course! He's my only son!

(Season 1, Episode 12, "Isabella")

TONY: See over there? Guy in there killed your father.

CHRISTOPHER: What the fuck are you talkin' about?

TONY: Barry Haydu. Detective Lieutenant in the Clifton Police Force. Retired today. That's his retirement party.

CHRISTOPHER: Everybody always told me it was a fuckin' cop. I thought he was dead. My mother can't even talk about it.

TONY: Did the hit for Jilly Rufalo. Jilly and your old man were in the can together. Jilly stabbed your old man's cellmate to death. So when your old man got paroled . . . he tracked down Jilly. Took out his eye so bad he couldn't even put a glass one in. Loyal, your old man.

CHRISTOPHER: That's what I heard. Some guy's eye. They hit my dad right outside my house, right? He was bringin' home a crib for me?

TONY: Yeah. Well no, he was outside the house but he wasn't carryin' a crib. He had a bunch of TV trays. Coulda been a crib just as easily. That rat fuck was in uniform then. Gambled like you wouldn't believe. He did it on contract. Made a lotta money over the years.

CHRISTOPHER: So how come he's still fuckin' walkin'?

TONY: 'Cause he's been useful. But he's outlived it, as of his "cute" little ceremony this afternoon.

CHRISTOPHER: Is that him?! With the sombrero on?

TONY: No you can't tell from here. But maybe it—yeah, probably. Here. Nice house, apparently. They say he paid cash for it. Good luck.

(Season 4, Episode 1, "For All Debts Public and Private")

ALLISON PAK: Mr. Soprano, Allison Pak, Channel Six.

JUNIOR: Allison, hi! [HITS HIS FACE ON A BIG MIKE, LOSES HIS BALANCE AND FALLS DOWN THE COURTHOUSE STEPS] Oh!

MELVOIN: Corrado!

OFFICER: Has he been shot?

MELVOIN: He got hit in the head by a boom.

ALLISON PAK: John, I'm here at the Federal Courthouse where reputed Mob boss, Corrado Soprano, just fell nine, no seven steps.

⊕   ⊕   ⊕   ⊕   ⊕

DR. WONG: [TO TONY] He was disoriented when he came in. Scored low on his Folstein. But that's consistent with concussion.

TONY: We're gonna sue the goddamn Justice Department!

DR. WONG: His CAT scan's negative, so, so far so good.

TONY: I don't know, he didn't seem like himself.

DR. WONG: A man his age, he could've been working on a dementia for quite a while and a blow to the head tipped him over.

TONY: You mean like Alzheimer's?

DR. WONG: That's one form of it.

⊕   ⊕   ⊕   ⊕   ⊕

TONY: You know, when you came in yesterday they said uh, you were very confused and you flunked your Holstein or somethin', I don't know.

JUNIOR: I'm 71 years old for Christ's sake. You get hit in the head, see how good you do.

TONY: I'm glad you're feelin' better.

JUNIOR: Better? This is Xanadu compared to that courtroom. I'm milkin' this thing for all it's worth.

TONY: Maybe you're not milkin' it enough.

JUNIOR: What?

TONY: You don't by any chance have any headaches, or blurred vision, or any of that shit, do ya?

⊕   ⊕   ⊕   ⊕   ⊕

MELVOIN: Our psychiatrist will testify as to your reduced mental capacity. Of course, the government will bring in their own expert.

TONY: Now, we get you 24-hour-a-day nursin' care, because they still didn't rule out the dementia . . . and uh, you might be a danger to yourself and uh, blah, blah, blah.

MELVOIN: Which only bolsters our case. If the court finds you lack fitness to proceed . . . the trial will be suspended and the charges against you dismissed with prejudice . . . or delayed.

TONY: I called this woman, she runs an elder care agency. She's got an RN that'll play ball. So all you gotta do is act oobatz.

JUNIOR: Crazy like a fox, my little nephew. Now get me the fuck outta here.

(Season 4, Episode 9, "Whoever Did This")

RALPH: Hadda be Paulie who told Johnny.

EUGENE: You think so?

RALPH: He hates my success. I keep thinkin' about that birthday dinner. Who was there when I told the Ginny Sack joke?

VITO: Not Paulie. I remember Albert sayin' he didn't get a gift.

RALPH: It was Little Paulie, the witless fuckin' nephew. He told Paulie, Paulie tells Johnny—fuckin' telephone game like high-school girls! You wanna play phone games? That party was the only time I ever mentioned Shamu's fat ass. [PICKS UP PHONE] Hello, Verona, Green Grove Retirement Home somethin' . . . just connect me.

EUGENE: Fuck you doin'?

RALPH: Yeah . . . hello? I'd like to talk to a Mrs. Gualtieri, she's a resident there.

NUCCI: Hello?

RALPH: Is this Marianuccia Gualtieri?

NUCCI: Yes.

RALPH: Hi, this is Detective Mike Hunt, Beaver Falls Pennsylvania Police Department. You have a son, Peter Paul?

NUCCI: Oh my God. What happened?

RALPH: He's all right, ma'am but I'm afraid he's in a little trouble. We found him in a public men's room in Lafayette Park. I don't know how to put this delicately . . . he was sucking a cub scout's dick.

NUCCI: What!? No, it's a mistake!

RALPH: Ma'am, I wish that was all . . . But I'm afraid we had to have emergency surgery performed upon arrival at headquarters after discovery of a small rodent in the rectal passage.

NUCCI: Oh, my God!

RALPH: A gerbil, ma'am. The County does not cover medical procedures deemed caused by criminal sexual activity . . . Section 4, Paragraph 15. We'll need an insurance number.

NUCCI: Oh, madonn'. I have Blue Cross Blue Shield, is that all right?

RALPH: Ma'am, could you hold on for one second? I have the hospital on the other line.

(Season 4, Episode 9, "Whoever Did This")

A Man Who Justifies His Actions

A man who justifies his actions isn't respected.

Tao Te Ching ☯ 24

PUSSY: There was a fuckin' rat. So you finger me? You think I didn't realize what was goin' on when you come to my house three o'clock in the fuckin' afternoon tellin' me you're my friend? That's when I knew I was in trouble, Anthony. When out of the blue you come and for no reason you start tellin' me you're my friend!

TONY: You owe me the fuckin' explanation! And you know what I'm talkin' about!

PUSSY: Yeah. Well, remind me, Tony, never to get sick again, huh? Remind me, please, never to have a serious illness because with you and Silvio and Paulie and all you pricks . . . weakness can spread as fuckin' treason!

(Season 2, Episode 1, "Guy Walks into a Psychiatrist's Office")

TONY: So that's it. Albert splits Nutley with the D'Alessio brothers and Barone here keeps everything north of Patterson. What else we gonna talk about?

DICK: Fairfield township's takin' bids next week.

RICHIE: What's there to talk about? Fairfield's mine.

TONY: Was yours. I don't give bids to the handicapped. See, obviously, Richie you're fuckin' deaf. Because I told you ten times. Then I find out you're still dealin' blow on those garbage routes.

RICHIE: For that I'm losing a fuckin' bid?

TONY: Next time you'll find yourself in back of one of your trucks.

JACKIE JR.: Those were my father's garbage routes!

RICHIE: Ssh, kid.

ALBERT: Actually, fellas, my cousin Larry wants the Fairfield contract. Bein' the hardship on his family and whatnot while he's in jail awaitin' trial.

TONY: See? This is why we have a fixed bid club. 'Cause everybody's got a story about why they should go to the head of the line.

RICHIE: I been in line for ten fuckin' years.

JACKIE JR.: My uncle's just asking for what my father would have given him if he was boss when Richie got out of prison. And it had nothin' to do with that they were brothers. You respected my father, you should respect Richie.

TONY: Those who want respect . . . give respect.

RICHIE: [TO JACKIE JR.] See, he just told you to shut the fuck up . . . and he told me to go fuck myself.

(Season 2, Episode 12, "Knight in White Satin Armor")

CHRISTOPHER: Bullshit. You're a fuckin' hypocrite.

TONY: What the fuck did you say?

CHRISTOPHER: You preach all this wiseguy shit and meanwhile the only ones who gotta play by the rules are us. I loved you.

TONY: What happens / decide, not you. Now you don't love me any-more, well that breaks my heart but it's too fuckin' bad. 'Cause you don't gotta love me. But you will respect me.

(Season 3, Episode 12, "Amour Fou")

ALBERT: What's with Ralph? Fuckin' Bermuda Triangle?

SILVIO: This shit with his kid. He's probably down in the bunker.

ALBERT: I'll tell ya . . . If I didn't know better . . .

SILVIO: We're off the record here, Albert.

ALBERT: We're off the record? It's Tony. What? Am I wrong?

SILVIO: Honestly? I don't know. Gonna take a leak.

ALBERT: This is bad, my friend. I mean, don't get me wrong. I wouldn't piss on this Ralph if he was on fire. But to whack a guy over a horse? How fucked up is that? If it can happen to him, it could happen to any of us. And what's next? You get clipped for wearin' the wrong shoes?

PATSY: What can you do? Tony's the boss. Centuries of tradition here.

ALBERT: Exactly my point. If Tony did do this—whack Ralph, over a fuckin' horse. That guy'd be the first guy on line to pull his fuckin' plug.

(Season 4, Episode 10, "The Strong, Silent Type")

TONY: Look, Carmine. You basically know what's goin' on with your dad and John and us over in Jersey.

LITTLE CARMINE: First let me say, I understand. And I appreciate the respect you're showin' me by comin' down here and reaching out to me at this time.

TONY: Always.

LITTLE CARMINE: And I will also go on record as sayin', "I know my old man can be a tough nut to crack."

TONY: I don't wanna crack nuts. But I will.

LITTLE CARMINE: I feel the anger.

TONY: When I try for the second time, on a separate issue entirely, to reach an accommodation, and he don't even make me a counter offer—where is his respect?

LITTLE CARMINE: I have no way of knowin' what kind of advice he's gettin' from Johnny.

TONY: Johnny's always usually a voice of moderation. Me and him, we get along good. So, all due respect, let's not jump in and blame Johnny.

LITTLE CARMINE: True. John's a pragmatist. But he's also a greedy motherfucker.

TONY: He lives above his head a little.

LITTLE CARMINE: I am reminded of Louis the whatever's finance minister, De-somethin'. He built a chateau. Nicole and I saw it when we went to Paris. It even outshone Versailles . . . where the king lived. In the end . . . Louis clapped him in irons.

(Season 4, Episode 11, "Calling All Cars")

Savoring the Moment

For all things there is a time for going ahead,
And a time for following behind;
A time for slow-breathing and a time for fast-breathing;
A time to grow in strength and a time to decay;
A time to be up and a time to be down.

Tao Te Ching ☯ 29

JUNIOR: I thought you were gonna ask my advice about Ralph Cifaretto.

TONY: Got any thoughts?

JUNIOR: What else do I have left? Real contretemps you have on your hands here. A good kid, but you never shoulda put Gigi in there.

TONY: Strong. Good earner. Well respected.

JUNIOR: Not by that crew. To them he's a Ghibelline comin' over to butt in. They don't trust him. They undermine him. On top of that you got Ralph now pissin' in their ears. Any day you'll have a mutiny on your hands.

TONY: So I take Gigi out. What kind of message does that send?

JUNIOR: That you're indecisive and unsure of yourself.

TONY: Exactly. Who the fuck would I replace him with anyway?

JUNIOR: All good questions.

TONY: Great. What's the fuckin' answer?

JUNIOR: Who says there is one? That's what being a boss is. You steer the ship the best way you know. Sometimes it's smooth, sometimes you hit the rocks. In the meantime, you find your pleasures where you can.

(Season 3, Episode 8, "He Is Risen")

TONY AND GEORGE: Fumble! Fumble!

REFEREE: Up! Up! Everybody up! Wait, get up.

TONY: Yeah! Yeah! That's A.J.! Yeah! Yeah! Good job, A.J.!

GOODWIN: Hey, good job, good job. Yeah!

TONY: Hey! Hey! That's my son. You got a nose for the ball, A.J., and that can't be taught.

ANTHONY JR.: Oh.

TONY: But a defensive lineman, you gotta have leverage and you gotta have footwork. I remember staying after practice every day, hittin' that sled till my shoulder was raw. But then you gotta reward yourself. So I'm gonna take you to Stewart's and I'll buy you some dogs.

ANTHONY JR.: I just wanna go home.

TONY: You should be riding high after what you did on the field today. C'mon!

ANTHONY JR.: Wanna play some Nintendo? You and me?

TONY: When're you gonna throw that friggin' thing out the friggin' window?

ANTHONY JR.: Why?

TONY: Well, all right. Play Nintendo.

ANTHONY JR.: Okay, let's go to Stewart's.

TONY: Yeah?

ANTHONY JR.: Yeah.

(Season 3, Episode 3, "Fortunate Son")

JACK: You don't have to answer this if you don't want to, but I gotta know. Did you ever meet John Gotti?

TONY: Yeah. I knew John.

RANDY: Whoa, fuck!

BRUCE: What was he really like?

TONY: Remember Bungalow Bar?

RANDY: The ice cream trucks?

BRUCE: Like Good Humor. Except the trucks, they had the bungalow roofs on 'em?

JACK: Was Gotti a silent partner in all that thing?

TONY: Hey, I don't know nothin' about that. Just know that when the company folded, and they were auctionin' off the last Bungalow Bar truck . . . and I wanted it as a souvenir, Gotti outbid me. He gave me a ride home. You know, he rang that bell the whole way home.

(Season 1, Episode 10, "A Hit Is a Hit")

When Exotic Goods
Are Traded

When exotic goods are traded and treasured,
The compulsion to steal is felt.

Tao Te Ching ☯ 3

SILVIO: Hey, Ton'. Sorry you have to wreck your Saturday like this.

TONY: You boys. You boys, I'll tell ya. It's beautiful stuff, though.

BRENDAN: Ton', I'm so sorry.

TONY: Shut up.

CHRISTOPHER: Just so long as you realize I had nothin' to do with this, Ton'.

BRENDAN: Ton', that's true. He stood home.

TONY: Shut up. Stood home? Did you do anything to stop it? Did you offer any guidance? What do we mean when we say leadership?

BRENDAN: Ton', part of it's the crank. You know, but I'm goin' into detox, swear on my mother.

CHRISTOPHER: Brendan, shut the fuck up. Do you want to get me clipped? What are we gonna do?

TONY: What you're gonna do is you're gonna take these suits, you're gonna put 'em back in the truck, you're gonna go over to Comley's main yard and you're gonna give 'em back.

CHRISTOPHER: Aw, fuck.

TONY: And then you're gonna call my uncle and you're gonna tell him when it's done.

CHRISTOPHER: What about the dead guy?

TONY: You keep proddin' him with a stick. You light a candle to St. Anthony. But I think you're fucked.

SILVIO: Ton', what if this didn't go back? Would it be a problem?

TONY: You know, I don't see you assholes puttin' that rack and that rack and this rack back in the truck.

SILVIO: Just when I thought I was out, they pull me back in.

(Season 1, Episode 2, "46 Long")

ADRIANA: Since you been, you know, "in," I just can't believe the stuff we get. It's so great.

CHRISTOPHER: Except for that spaccone Paulie. Fuck him and the Coupe Deville he rode in on.

(Season 3, Episode 7, "Second Opinion")

CHRISTOPHER: Hey, Ton', sorry I'm late. What's up?

TONY: You tell me. Got a call from Jack Massarone. Massarone Construction? A very angry call.

CHRISTOPHER: The M-80 in the porta-pot. I fuckin' told Benny—

TONY: Don't fuck with me on this.

CHRISTOPHER: Fiber optic shit.

TONY: So you knew it was gonna be boosted?

CHRISTOPHER: No. Well, yeah, I mean . . . Patsy mentioned some—

TONY: Aw Jesus Christ, if I wanted Patsy in charge . . . Use your fuckin' head, Christopher.

CHRISTOPHER: I'm sorry, T, I thought I was.

TONY: By drawin' heat to a quarter billion dollar job? Think, Christopher, think. The big fuckin' picture, huh?

CHRISTOPHER: Aren't they insured?

(Season 4, Episode 2, "No-Show")

SILVIO: What'd you want?

PATSY: Nothin', really. But you should see the floor tiles, though. That got delivered to the job site? Mexican travertine.

SILVIO: Johnny Sposato'll take that shit.

PATSY: No more dippin' at the job according to fuckin' Alfalfa. But the order . . . comes down from Tony.

SILVIO: Go ahead.

PATSY: What? Knock off the tile? Tony says "no."

SILVIO: I got your back. Tony'll be fine with it.

(Season 4, Episode 2, "No-Show")

An Excessive Love

An excessive love for anything
Will cost you dear in the end.

Tao Te Ching ☯ 44

TONY: [GOING INTO MRI] You think I got a brain tumor?

CARMELA: Well, we're gonna find out.

TONY: What a bedside manner. Very encouraging.

CARMELA: What, are you gonna not know?

TONY: We had some good times. Had some good years.

CARMELA: Here he goes now with the nostalgia.

TONY: Hey, all I'm sayin' is no marriage is perfect.

CARMELA: Well havin' that goomar on the side helps.

TONY: I told you, I'm not seein' her anymore. How do you think I feel havin' that priest around all the time?

CARMELA: Don't even go there, all right? Father is a spiritual mentor. He's helpin' me to be a better Catholic!

TONY: Yeah, well we all got different needs.

CARMELA: What's different between you and me is you're goin' to hell when you die!

(Season 1, Episode 1, "Pilot")

TONY: Dr. Melfi, there's nothin' there, you know.

CARMELA: You don't have to explain nothin', Tony.

TONY: This psychiatrist shit . . . apparently what you're feelin' is not what you're feelin'. And what you're not feelin' is your real agenda.

CARMELA: You're gonna stick with it, right?

TONY: I don't know.

CARMELA: I think you should.

TONY: You do?

CARMELA: I was jealous.

TONY: I shoulda told you . . .

CARMELA: No, wait, let me finish, Tony. I've been thinkin' a lot about this . . . I was jealous of her ability to help you. To be a sort of salvation to you. I talked to Father Phil and . . . I want to be that woman in your life.

TONY: Carm, you're not just in my life . . . you are my life. Come here.

(Season 1, Episode 6, "Pax Soprana")

BOBBI: Who would've ever thought we could've been this contented?

JUNIOR: I did. As soon as I saw you, I knew.

BOBBI: You're a sweetheart. If only they knew the other side of you.

JUNIOR: They'd eat me for breakfast.

BOBBI: How's Junior Junior? Hm?

JUNIOR: He's catchin' some shut-eye.

BOBBI: You're such a powerhouse. When you kiss me down there, you're like a great artist. You got a real instinct for it.

JUNIOR: Pass me the red peppers.

BOBBI: You know the thrill you give?

JUNIOR: Just keep it to yourself, okay, Roberta?

BOBBI: Yeah, all to myself. Corrado?

JUNIOR: Yeah?

BOBBI: Why the big secret?

JUNIOR: About what?

BOBBI: Oral sex. What's so terrible about pleasin' a woman?

JUNIOR: You always have to talk about everything.

BOBBI: Well, I wanna know why!

JUNIOR: It's complicated.

BOBBI: Yeah. But, why?

JUNIOR: Why? Because they think if you suck pussy, you'll suck anything.

BOBBI: Oh, you're kidding?

JUNIOR: It's a sign of weakness. And possibly a sign that you're a finooch'.

BOBBI: A fag? That's ridiculous . . . How would the two even translate?

JUNIOR: What're ya gonna do, I mean, I don't make the rules.

(Season 1, Episode 9, "Boca")

TONY: This better be good, I was takin' my kid fishin'.

VIN: Ah, Jesus. What? No "How you been, how's it doin', Vin, what-dya think, Vin"?

TONY: I thought we understood each other, right? I don't give two shits about your family, or whether you take it up the ass. Now what's so important you take me away from my boat? Hey, fuck face, where are you goin'?

VIN: Why you gotta talk to me like this, I do a lot of risky shit for you.

TONY: Yeah, you're not doin' charity work, remember? All right, I'm sorry. Vin, howya doin'? Whatya got for me?

VIN: Bonpensiero.

TONY: Pussy? What about him?

VIN: He's wired for sound.

TONY: What?

VIN: I got it from a good source, I thought you should know. All right? I'm sorry, I know you like him.

TONY: Like him? I fuckin' *love* him. Now who's your source?

VIN: He's on the force, he's on the task force, all right? Look, he's not lyin' to me, he was in my wedding.

TONY: I wanna see the report.

VIN: I can't get my hands . . .

TONY: I wanna see the fuckin' 302!

VIN: All right, all right. I'll see what I can do.

TONY: It doesn't make any sense.

VIN: Yeah it does, Ton', if you take the blinders off. I'm in robbery homicide and I was told he was movin' a lot of heavy H to pay for his kid's college. Why would I know somethin' like that? And last spring, in that big heroin bust, where was he? He told you he was in Las Vegas, am I right? All right, again, I'm sorry, but yeah, that's where he was, he was in Las Vegas, he was in a Federal building cuttin' a deal! And why did he walk so easy from that thing the other day? Known wiseguy resisted arrest, who walks away from a thing like that with lowball bail?

TONY: Why would he do it?

VIN: Why, because he's facin' a possible sentence of "from now on," mandatory, that's why. Come on, I know a lot of guys who can't do that kind of time. Who is this guy, Pussy, huh? Who is he, he's a man who loves his family above all else. Well guess what, that's their favorite target.

(Season 1, Episode 11, "Nobody Knows Anything")

CARMELA: So, Richie, you and Par—Janice . . . This is no flash in the pan.

RICHIE: Yeah, it's ironic how life works. I mean, she goes to Sri Lanka, or wherever . . . I go where I went and here we are back where we started twenty years ago.

CARMELA: For every shoe there is a mate.

(Season 2, Episode 8, "Full Leather Jacket")

CARMELA: Vic?

VIC: Carmela, hi!

CARMELA: Imagine running into you here! How are you?

VIC: Good. I'm fine. And how are you?

CARMELA: Good.

VIC: Yeah?

CARMELA: Just shoppin' for a roller.

VIC: Ah.

CARMELA: Look, Vic. Truthfully, I'm not just running into you here. I saw the name of the store on your supplies . . . I wanted to talk to you.

VIC: Carmela, I'm sorry. I shoulda called you that day.

CARMELA: Please. You have nothing to be sorry for.

VIC: I shoulda called you and told you I wasn't coming for lunch.

CARMELA: That's all right. I got the message when you didn't show up. And that's why I wanted to talk to you. I wanted to thank you.

VIC: For what?

CARMELA: Maybe someday I will be free. But if you had come that day I might have done something that I would be sorry for forever. And so I wanted to thank you for thinking for the both of us. Being strong for the both of us.

⊕   ⊕   ⊕   ⊕   ⊕

CARMELA: Goddamn him!

GABRIELLA: They're all the same, Carm.

CARMELA: No, you know they're not. That man who did my wallpaper. There was a male person that you could respect and . . .

GABRIELLA: Victor Musto? Carmela, he didn't show up that day because of who your husband is. Face it, use your head. He pissed his pants.

(Season 2, Episode 12, "The Knight in White Satin Armor")

SVETLANA: Irina, a man is here to see you.

IRINA: Who?

SVETLANA: The one who has the club. Mr. Dante.

SILVIO: How ya doin', hon?

IRINA: Who sended you, Tony?

SILVIO: Yeah, he asked me to bring you this.

IRINA: What is it, money? I don't want it.

SILVIO: Yes, you do. There's seventy-five thousand dollars in here.

IRINA: Seventy-five?

SILVIO: Listen. Irina, I know you're upset. But let me give you a little . . . advice. In my business I see girls come and go. So I know. Time is the great enemy. You've got a very short window. It's not good to get too hung up on any one thing. On the other hand, something new always comes along. I've seen it a million times. It's called passages. You know, it's a book.

SVETLANA: He's right, Irinushka. He's very smart man.

(Season 2, Episode 12, "The Knight in White Satin Armor")

TONY: [ABOUT ADRIANA] What the fuck is wrong with you? She's his fuckin' fiancée!

ARTIE: I loved her. I fuckin' love her now.

TONY: Artie, do me a favor. Don't ever fuckin' say that again to anybody ever.

ARTIE: What am I, a joke?

TONY: Yeah, a stupid fuckin' bald one. Not to mention married, hmm?

ARTIE: Can I tell you somethin'? She's a cunt. My fuckin' wife . . . A girl like Ade, that's a woman. If I still had my hair . . .

TONY: Artie, she's a young girl. You could have hair like fuckin' Casey Kasem, it wouldn't make a difference.

(Season 3, Episode 5, "Another Toothpick")

RALPH: Where's Tony?

GIGI: Gettin' his weasel greased.

(Season 3, Episode 6, "University," p. 47)

RALPH: Women, women, women. Why was I born handsome instead of rich?

TRACEE: Leave me alone.

RALPH: What's the matter with you? What are you bein' like this for?

TRACEE: Fuck you. Three days you don't call, even to see how I am.

RALPH: Baby, I'm *busy*, I gotta work. How else am I gonna take care of you when you're nine months pregnant?

TRACEE: You serious?

RALPH: Of course, I'm serious. We'll get a little house. In a cul de sac. I know that guy who's a mortgage broker.

TRACEE: Really? Ralphie . . . I love you.

RALPH: I love you too, baby. Hey . . . if it's a boy, we'll name him after me. If it's a girl, we'll name her Tracee after you. This way she can grow up to be a cock-suckin' slob just like her mother.

(Season 3, Episode 6, "University")

TONY: [ABOUT GLORIA] Me and this broad we're like . . . leather and lace. Burning ring of fire. Whatever the fuck.

DR. MELFI: Amour fou. As the French call it. Crazy love, all-consuming.

TONY: That's it. I tell ya, we push each other's buttons.

(Season 3, Episode 12, "Amour Fou")

DR. MELFI: Why are you so attracted to dangerous relationships? Why do you put your marriage in such danger?

TONY: Maybe I'm lookin' for a way out. Ever think of that?

DR. MELFI: Anthony . . . you'll never leave your wife.

TONY: Bullshit. You know there's a limit to how much shit—

DR. MELFI: She might leave you, but you'll never leave her. Despite your mothering, you made one good decision in your life vis-à-vis women. You're not gonna throw that over. Your own selfishness is too strong to let that happen.

(Season 3, Episode 12, "Amour Fou")

JUNIOR: There she is.

NURSE: You be good now, don't start.

JUNIOR: You oughta see my finish.

NURSE: You know you could sue for talk like that nowadays.

JUNIOR: Then cancel my appointment. Let me die now if a man can't voice to a beautiful woman the zephyrs that are blowing through his mind.

NURSE: My God, will you listen to him today? Go in there now and strip down to your shorts.

JUNIOR: Ya see now? I'm not gonna touch that line. Too much class. But as for that lovely laugh line . . .

NURSE: Come on handsome, we're busy.

JUNIOR: Give me that cheek . . . right here. I surrender. Do with me what you will.

(Season 4, Episode 1, "For All Debts Public and Private")

CHRISTOPHER: What is it with you and this girl?

ADRIANA: What, I can't have friends?

CHRISTOPHER: You're amazing, you know that? With all your intelligence you never see the big picture. You met her where?

ADRIANA: At the mall. So?

CHRISTOPHER: Think, Adriana, think. Girl like that. Ass like that. And she don't have a boyfriend, she don't like Paulie.

ADRIANA: Oh, like he's Jude Law.

CHRISTOPHER: Yeah, whatever. Are you that fuckin' blind? She's a dyke.

(Season 4, Episode 2, "No-Show")

DEBORAH: She's really gonna marry him? What is wrong with this girl?

AGENT HARRIS: Come on. Moltisanti's a great catch. Tall, dark and sociopathic.

(Season 4, Episode 7, "Watching Too Much Television")

MAURIZIO: My brother lived a full life, he had lots of women.

FURIO: That's the best you can hope for.

MAURIZIO: You gonna stay around awhile?

FURIO: Since I left for America, all I thought about was coming back here. When I saw Naples from the airplane I got a hard-on.

MAURIZIO: What do you expect? It's home.

FURIO: I don't know anymore. Even the San Gennaro Cathedral. I went to pray for my father. There were hamburger wrappers everywhere . . .

MAURIZIO: I don't think it's litter that's got you turned around.

FURIO: There's a woman.

MAURIZIO: So go home to her. You did the duties of a son.

FURIO: She's the don's wife.

MAURIZIO: Soprano?

FURIO: He doesn't know.

MAURIZIO: You fucking her?

FURIO: I'm not even sure that she knows. I never even kissed her.

MAURIZIO: Good, so you stay away. No harm done.

FURIO: I don't know if I can. I love her.

MAURIZIO: You fucking crazy? All the shit I pulled in my life, I never fucked the boss's wife. You know why? You know why?

FURIO: Stop the rhetorical questions.

MAURIZIO: Because I know he would kill me if he found out. And they always find out everything, these bosses. [ANSWERS PHONE] Hello? Hold on. I have to take this. My lawyer. The only way you could have her is if you killed the man.

FURIO: I know this.

MAURIZIO: Eh. So? Don't be an idiot.

(Season 4, Episode 8, "Mergers and Acquisitions")

CARMELA: So, uh, aside from your dad, was it wonderful being back in Italy?

FURIO: Oh, it was wonderful, yeah.

CARMELA: Go home, see your friends, your family.

FURIO: I gotta be honest. It was not so nice. I don't belong there no more.

CARMELA: No?

FURIO: Something change. Maybe me.

CARMELA: What do you mean?

FURIO: I'm like visitor in my own town. Life went on without me. There is nothing there for me now.

CARMELA: No special someone?

FURIO: I feel strange to live here also. Maybe I should never have come to America.

CARMELA: You've made such a nice life for yourself, though. You've got a wonderful home. A girlfriend.

FURIO: No.

CARMELA: No? What do you mean, no? Jessica?

FURIO: I tried to talk to her, but, there is no communication. Like with some people, you know what I mean?

CARMELA: That's what love is built on.

FURIO: Si.

CARMELA: So, why did you come back?

(Season 4, Episode 10, "The Strong, Silent Type")

CARMELA: I was so upset when he didn't bring me a present back from Italy. He got somethin' for A.J. and for Meadow. He did give me some vinegar but I don't think it was meant for me. It musta meant somethin' that he felt bad.

ROSALIE: Carmela, you sound like you're fifteen years old.

CARMELA: I say I'm helpin' him decorate. I bring A.J. with me. Now even he smells a rat.

ROSALIE: Carmela, if Tony suspects one iota you know what'll happen to Furio—these guys are livin' in a different century.

CARMELA: It didn't stop you.

ROSALIE: Steve at the gym? I felt so guilty all the time. The lies, and the sneaking. It took Jackie goin' in the hospital to get me to stop.

CARMELA: We haven't slept together yet.

ROSALIE: You're not fuckin' him? So this isn't really real.

CARMELA: It is real. We communicate. He looks at me like I'm beautiful. He thinks I'm interesting when I talk. Just those few minutes when we see each other—I live for those. I feel like my life is slippin' through my fingers and I will never be happy.

ROSALIE: If you haven't slept with him yet, don't. And don't go over there anymore.

(Season 4, Episode 10, "The Strong, Silent Type")

CARMELA: You know what, Tony? What's done is done. We are where we are, it's for the best, but just for the record, or it might even interest you to know that I might actually have gone on, with your cheating and your bullshit if your attitude around here had been even the least bit loving, cooperative, interested . . .

TONY: Whose idea was Whitecaps?

CARMELA: It's just a bigger version of an emerald ring. So you can keep on with your other life.

TONY: You don't know me at all.

CARMELA: I know you better than anybody, Tony. Even your friends. Which is probably why you hate me.

TONY: Hate you? Well, don't worry, I'm going to hell when I die. Nice thing to say to a person heading into an MRI.

CARMELA: You know, Tony, I have always been sorry I said that. You were my guy. You could be so sweet. Nobody could make me laugh like you.

TONY: Carmela, who the fuck did you think I was when you married me, huh? You knew my father. You grew up around Dickie Moltisanti and your uncle Eddie. Where do you get off acting all surprised and miffed when there are women on the side? You knew the deal.

CARMELA: Deal?

TONY: And your mother can talk all she wants about what's his name and his fuckin' chain of drugstores . . . you and I both know that the other boyfriend you were debating marryin' was Jerry Tufi, with his father's snowplow business. And we now know that that wouldn't have suited you at all.

CARMELA: You really don't hear me, do you? You think for me it's all about things.

TONY: No, I forced all this shit on you. What you really crave is a little Hyundai and a simple gold heart on a chain.

CARMELA: You are so fucking hateful. Can I tell you something, Tony?

TONY: Don't pretend like I got a choice.

CARMELA: The last year . . . I have been dreaming and fantasizing and in love with Furio.

TONY: What?

CARMELA: Every morning when he'd come to pick you up, I would look forward to it all night long, in bed next to you. Those nights when you were actually in the bed. And he would ring the doorbell, I felt like my heart would come out of my chest. He would smile and we'd talk . . . and then you would come down the stairs. And I felt probably like someone who is terminally ill and somehow they manage to forget it for a minute . . . and then it all comes back.

(Season 4, Episode 13, "Whitecaps")

The Farther You Go

The farther you go,
The less you know.

Tao Te Ching ☯ **47**

TONY: [ON CELLPHONE] The guy you're looking for is some kind of ex-commando or some shit. He killed sixteen Chechen rebels single-handed.

PAULIE: [ON CELLPHONE] T? T, that you?

TONY: Goddamnit.

PAULIE: I didn't hear what you said, Ton'.

TONY: It's a bad connection, so I'm gonna talk fast! The guy you're looking for is an ex-commando! He killed sixteen Chechen rebels single-handed!

PAULIE: Get the fuck outta here.

TONY: Yeah, nice, huh? He was with the Interior Ministry. Guy's some kind of Russian Green Beret. This guy cannot come back to tell this story. You understand?

PAULIE: I hear you.

TONY: I'm fuckin' serious, Paulie.

PAULIE: Ton'? Ton', you there?

TONY: Goddamn! Fuck! Call me back!

PAULIE: [TO CHRISTOPHER] You're not gonna believe this. He killed sixteen Czechoslovakians. The guy was an interior decorator.

CHRISTOPHER: His house looked like shit.

(Season 3, Episode 11, "Pine Barrens")

TONY: What the fuck's in Europe?

CARMELA: Experience. Real life. Art.

TONY: You know, I knew all this constant harpin' on art was gonna cause trouble.

(Season 4, Episode 2, "No-Show")

TONY: You wanna go to Europe? Go. Clear your head. Run with the bulls. Do whatever it is the hell they do over there.

MEADOW: Thank you, I will.

CARMELA: Don't you think she should talk to someone first? A counselor, maybe?

TONY: Maybe the college of hard knocks is what she needs. And let's see how she likes it when some gypsy lifts her wallet. Let her find out you can't work over there without a permit, which the French hang onto like their balls.

(Season 4, Episode 2, "No-Show")

Not Knowing Is
True Knowledge

Not knowing is true knowledge.

Tao Te Ching ☯ **71**

DR. MELFI: I don't know where this story is going. But there are a few ethical ground rules we should quickly get out of the way. What you tell me here falls under doctor/patient confidentiality. Except if I was uh, if I was to hear let's say a murder was to take place, not that I'm saying it would, but if. If a patient comes to me and tells me a story where someone's going to get hurt, I'm supposed to go to the authorities . . . Technically. You said you were in waste management.

TONY: The environment.

(Season 1, Episode 1, "Pilot")

MEADOW: Are you in the Mafia?

TONY: Am I in the what?

MEADOW: Whatever you want to call it—organized crime?

TONY: That's total crap. Who told you that?

MEADOW: Dad, I've lived in the house all my life. I've seen police come with warrants, I've seen you going out at three in the morning.

TONY: So, you never seen Doc Cusamano go out at three in the morning on a call?

MEADOW: Did the Cusamano kids ever find fifty thousand dollars in Krugerrands and a .45 automatic while they were hunting for Easter eggs?

TONY: I'm in the waste management business, everybody immediately assumes you're mobbed up. It's a stereotype, and it's offensive. And you're the last person I would want to perpetuate it.

MEADOW: Fine.

TONY: There is no Mafia. All right, look . . . Med, you're a grown woman—almost. Some of my money comes from illegal gamblin' and what-not. How does that make you feel?

MEADOW: At least you don't keep denying it like Mom. The kids in school think it's actually kind of neat.

TONY: As in "The Godfather," right?

MEADOW: Not really. "Casino"-y, like, Sharon Stone—the seventies clothes, pills.

TONY: I'm not askin' about those bums. I'm askin' about you.

MEADOW: Sometimes I wish you were like other dads. But then like, Mr. Scangarelo, for example . . . an advertising executive for big tobacco, or lawyers, ugh. So many dads are full of shit.

TONY: And I'm not.

MEADOW: You finally told the truth about this.

TONY: Look, Med, part of my income comes from legitimate business. You know, the stock market, I . . .

MEADOW: Look, Dad, please okay. Don't start mealy-mouthing.

(Season 1, Episode 5, "College")

CARMELA: Meadow, honey, you should have been workin' this summer. If only to feel good about yourself. Get your mind off of Jackie, instead of layin' out by that pool.

MEADOW: I read, Mom. Out by that pool. Probably half the canon.

CARMELA: The canon. Okay, what is that now?

MEADOW: Now? The great books? Western literature? Dead white males? Who even in their reductionism have quite interesting things to say about death and loss. Maybe more interesting than what you have to say.

CARMELA: Is Mary Higgins Clark a part of that group, 'cause that's what I saw you reading every time I passed by the pool.

(Season 4, Episode 2, "No-Show")

DEBORAH: That's a search warrant. Your office, your club, your cocaine.

ADRIANA: It's not my cocaine.

DEBORAH: Really? That's not what I have you saying on tape.

ADRIANA: You were fuckin' tapin' me?

DEBORAH: If I were you? I'd put aside my hurt feelings for a while.

ADRIANA: I told you shit in confidence that had nothin' to do with any of this shit! Things that I never told no one.

DEBORAH: They're offering you a way out, Ade. A chance to save your life and Christopher's life.

ADRIANA: You don't give a fuck about us. You and your fuckin' OB/GYN doctor. You just wanted me and Christopher to stay together long enough so you could find shit out.

CUBITOSO: We understand your fiancé is moving up in the world. Or down, as the case may be.

HARRIS: Problems at the Esplanade construction site.

ADRIANA: Oh my God.

CUBITOSO: We're not asking you to wear a wire. We're not asking you to testify. We just want information.

ADRIANA: [TO DEBORAH] Is your name even Danielle? What if I say no?

CUBITOSO: If you say no . . . you'll be placed under arrest, and charged with possession and intent to distribute cocaine. A charge that carries with it a penalty of up to twenty-five years in prison.

ADRIANA: Oh, my God.

HARRIS: And after you make bail you could explain to Tony Soprano why you brought an undercover federal agent into his home during Sunday dinner.

ADRIANA: My God.

DEBORAH: We'll probably never hear about it, though.

ADRIANA: Oh my God . . . [SOBBING]

DEBORAH: Chances are you and Christopher will just disappear.

[ADRIANA VOMITS]

CUBITOSO: Get the wastebasket.

(Season 4, Episode 2, "No-Show")

CARMELA: Did you get any sleep?

MEADOW: A little, I think.

CARMELA: Maybe it would be better if you went back to school. Got your head into your schoolwork. Be with your friends.

MEADOW: I'd just be thinking about what's going on here all the time. I just keep thinking . . . I used to feel so superior 'cause so many of my friends had these fucked-up divorced parents.

CARMELA: I guess I did, too.

MEADOW: And like Finn. I'm not saying I want kids, but if we did . . .

I used to imagine we'd all be together on the holidays, Christmas. All be around this big fire.

CARMELA: You will have a wonderful future, Meadow. We had a lot of wonderful times as a family.

MEADOW: All predicated on bullshit.

CARMELA: I don't want to fight with you, Meadow. That's not true. I think you know it.

MEADOW: It was 'cause of Furio, wasn't it?

CARMELA: Who said anything about Furio? I have never been unfaithful to your father.

MEADOW: Daddy was.

CARMELA: This is not something I want to talk about. I'm sorry. Not now, not ever.

MEADOW: Jesus, how could you eat shit from him for all those years?

(Season 4, Episode 13, "Whitecaps")

MEADOW: What's going on?

TONY: I was just tellin' everybody, it's probably better if I don't live here anymore.

ANTHONY JR.: 'Cause I wanted to stay in there with you? I won't ask. I just got pissed off.

CARMELA: [TO TONY] He asked to live with you?

TONY: [TO ANTHONY JR.] No, A.J. C'mere. That's not why.

MEADOW: Where are you gonna go?

TONY: Don't worry about it.

MEADOW: You should go back to counseling.

TONY: It's better this way.

CARMELA: He's making the right decision. He'll get a place, you will go and visit. It'll be better. You'll see.

ANTHONY JR.: Well, you guys could still get back together, maybe? Right?

TONY: Yeah. Sure. We're still close.

(Season 4, Episode 13, "Whitecaps")

If People Have Lives Worth Living

If people don't love life,
They won't fear death,
And threatening them with it won't work.
If people have lives worth living,
Then the threat of death is meaningful,
And they'll do what is right to avoid it.

Tao Te Ching ☯ **74**

BACALA: You're Teddy Genaretti, aren't ya? The shop steward for Local 184?

TEDDY: Guilty. Are you a joint fitter?

BARTENDER: What can I get you?

BACALA: Wild Turkey neat. I saw your Caravan in the lot. It's a nice car for a family.

TEDDY: Do I know you?

BACALA: Jim Blake.

TEDDY: What local you in?

BACALA: Bad back. It's just that I follow these things, you know, this election coming up. Dick Hoffman for president? I heard he's got 184's vote. I think it's a mistake.

TEDDY: Pension's been ripped off for the last twenty-five years.

BACALA: Hey, I'm sure you guys got grievances, but Dick Hoffman? What do you owe this guy? It's all talk. He's out of touch with reality, Dick. You think if push came to shove he'd give a fuck about you?

TEDDY: I know what you're tryin' to do.

BACALA: You look like a smart guy. I can see why your local puts their faith in you to do the right thing. I'm just saying, if it was me? I got kids that depend on me. Like yourself. And to waste my votes on somebody like Dick Hoffman? I might as well put a bullet in my head, here, here, and here.

(Season 4, Episode 5, "Pie-O-My")

The Five Colors
Blind the Eye

The five colors blind the eye.
The five tones deafen the ear.
The five flavors overwhelm the palate.

Tao Te Ching ☯ 12

FATHER PHIL: I also have a confession to make, Carm. I have a Jones for your baked ziti.

⊕   ⊕   ⊕   ⊕   ⊕

FATHER PHIL: Well, oh man, I better get goin'.

CARMELA: Where you goin'? You just got here.

FATHER PHIL: It's gettin' late.

CARMELA: But it's pourin' rain out. Oh, and I know you love that DVD player. I just got "Remains of the Day."

FATHER PHIL: Hmmm.

CARMELA: See, do I know you?

FATHER PHIL: Anything with Emma Thompson, I'm there.

CARMELA: Father Phil, I didn't know you looked.

FATHER PHIL: What? To take in through the eyes a beautiful woman . . . is that so different than a sunset? A Douglas fir? Or any of God's handiwork?

⊕   ⊕   ⊕   ⊕   ⊕

FATHER PHIL: Last night . . . we didn't do anything out of line?

CARMELA: There's nothing to apologize about.

FATHER PHIL: Right.

CARMELA: That's right.

FATHER PHIL: Ah, I should get dressed. Get goin'.

CARMELA: Anthony Jr. will be home soon.

FATHER PHIL: Oh, my God. My car's been out there all night in plain sight.

CARMELA: We didn't do anything wrong. Is there a commandment against eating ziti? It's okay, take a shower, get dressed. Don't forget your sacrament kit, whatever.

ANTHONY JR.: I'm home!

FATHER PHIL: Carmela . . . I don't know where to begin. See, it's not that I don't have desire for you in my heart.

CARMELA: Madonn', Father, please.

FATHER PHIL: But last night was one of the most difficult tests from God ever for me.

CARMELA: What are you talkin' about? We're friends.

FATHER PHIL: What's that look about?

CARMELA: What, I look some way? I was just thinking about when we watched "Casablanca" last week.

FATHER PHIL: That new print is great, huh?

CARMELA: You know when Bogie says "Of all the lousy gin joints in the world, why'd you have to pick mine?" Of all the finooch' priests in the world, why did I have to get the one who's straight?

FATHER PHIL: Carmela.

CARMELA: [LAUGHS] Come on, it's a joke.

(Season 1, Episode 5, "College")

TV NEWS VOICE: A strange and macabre Christmas story, another sad incidence of continuing violence against livery drivers. In downtown Newark, police were called to the scene of what appeared to be a Christmas prank gone awry. Livery driver Igor Parnasky was found trapped under Santa's sleigh and severely beaten inside the window display at Curran's Sporting Goods. The Russian émigré also suffered injuries from broken glass. From his description of his assailants, police are questioning members of a marauding youth gang known to call this part of Newark *their* turf.

JANICE: Oh my God. Oh . . .

TV NEWS VOICE: Merry Christmas. Reporting live from downtown Newark, this is Monica Perkins.

TV NEWS VOICE: Thank you, Monica. A family from Oklahoma . . .

JANICE: Oh, yeah . . . Aaron? Honey?

AARON: Yeah?

JANICE: I think I know what's missing from the song. It's the brother concept.

AARON: He ain't heavy?

JANICE: No, I mean not exactly. We just—maybe we can try to get something down.

AARON: Jan, you're cryin'.

JANICE: Sometimes we really don't see our loved ones.

(Season 3, Episode 10, "To Save Us All from Satan's Power")

To See the Small

To see the small is to have insight.

Tao Te Ching ☯ 52

DR. MELFI: [TO HER HUSBAND RICHARD] We all know you're a sucker for those Irish girls. Every Italian boy bows down to the freckles.

(Season 1, Episode 8, "The Legend of Tennessee Moltisanti")

CARMELA: Has Anna chosen her caterer yet?

ADRIANA: She booked Villa de Roma.

CARMELA: Good. 'Cause if you ask me, Caravaggio's is slipping.

ADRIANA: I heard they fired the produce guy.

CHRISTOPHER: Enough! I am so sick and tired of hearin' you people talk about food, food, food. That's all anybody ever talks about is prozhoot, cheese, and fuckin' favi beans! I'm drownin' here!

TONY: Jesus Christ, take it easy!

CHRISTOPHER: We're not even engaged yet!

TONY: Well, when you're married you'll understand the importance of fresh produce!

(Season 2, Episode 7, "D-Girl")

SILVIO: What the fuck you doing? Lunch is ready.

PAULIE: Wash my hands.

SILVIO: You just washed your hands.

PAULIE: Then I tied my shoe.

SILVIO: So what?

PAULIE: Well I can't stand touching fuckin' shoelaces. You ever go to tie your shoes and you notice the ends of your laces are wet? From what? Why would they be wet?

SILVIO: I got no fuckin' idea.

PAULIE: You go to public bathrooms? You stand at the urinal?

HESH: Aah, fuck, come on, will ya?

PAULIE: He's asking me, I'm telling him. And frankly, it's important. Even if the lace is dry and even if you don't touch the body of the shoe . . . Bacteria and virus migrate from the sole up.

CHRISTOPHER: You see this on TV?

PAULIE: I gotta watch TV to figure out the world? Your average men's shithouse is a fuckin' sewer. You look in ladies' johns, you could eat maple walnut ice cream from the toilets. Ah, there's exceptions. But a men's? Piss all over the fuckin' floor, urinals jammed with cigarettes and mothball cakes. And they can pour all the fuckin' ice they want down there, my friend, it does nothin' to kill germs. Even if you keep your shoes tied and you're not dragging your laces through urine . . .

SILVIO: Oh, shut the fuck up!

(Season 3, Episode 1, "Mr. Ruggerio's Neighborhood")

PAULIE: The amazing thing about snakes is that they reproduce spontaneously.

TONY: Whaddaya mean?

PAULIE: The have both male and female sex organs. That's why somebody you don't trust you call a snake. How can you trust a guy that can literally go fuck themselves?

TONY: Wouldn't you think that expression came from the Adam and Eve story, where the snake tempted Eve to go bite that apple?

PAULIE: Hey, snakes been fuckin' themselves long before Adam and Eve showed up.

(Season 3, Episode 9, "The Telltale Moozadell")

CARMINE: How's Junior?

TONY: He's gonna be all right.

CARMINE: Tell him he's in our prayers, etc.

TONY: I'll be sure and let him know.

CARMINE: One other thing, though. John said he went to a cookout at your house.

TONY: Yeah?

CARMINE: A don doesn't wear shorts.

(Season 4, Episode 1, "For All Debts Public and Private")

RAYMOND: I'll tell ya what a gold mine is, those Harry Potter books.

BACALA: That's 'cause it gives the other kids, the ninety-eight pound weaklings, some hope.

(Season 4, Episode 2, "No-Show")

PAULIE: How much to paint a different suit on him, change his face a little?

PRABHAT: Pardon me?

PAULIE: Why throw it away? A stronger chin maybe? I was thinkin' like those paintin's you see in the courthouse. Somethin' classy, you know, like a revolutionary war general. Napoleon and his horse. That kinda thing.

PRABHAT: He's rather portly to be Napoleon.

PAULIE: Not Napoleon exactly. *Like* Napoleon.

(Season 4, Episode 10, "The Strong, Silent Type")

Don't Leave a Trace

Good walking leaves no track behind it;
Good speech leaves no mark to be picked at;
Good calculation makes no use of counting-slips;
Good shutting makes no use of bolt and bar,
    And yet nobody can undo it;
Good tying makes no use of rope and knot,
    And yet nobody can untie it.

Tao Te Ching ☯ 27

PUSSY: You whacked this kid. You shoulda waited for me, Christopher.

CHRISTOPHER: The last time I show any fuckin' initiative. Can you imagine how I felt? T's runnin' down the garbage business, I just fuckin' wet a guy to hold down to one of our stops.

PUSSY: He's not running it down. It's just gettin' harder in New York. The Kolar uncle is gonna find the kid dead on one of his bins and get out of our fuckin' business? No way.

CHRISTOPHER: "Louis Brassi sleeps with the fishes."

PUSSY: Luca Brassi . . . Luca.

CHRISTOPHER: Whatever.

PUSSY: There's differences, Christopher, okay? From the Luca Brassi situation and this? Look, if the Kolars know the kid is dead, it hardens their position. Plus now, the cops are lookin' for a fuckin' murderer.

CHRISTOPHER: So what do you wanna do?

PUSSY: He disappears. He never comes home. They know, but they don't know. They hope maybe he'll turn up . . . "if."

(Season 1, Episode 1, "Pilot")

CHRISTOPHER: They say . . . there's no two people on earth exactly the same. No two faces, no two sets of fingerprints. But do they know that for sure? 'Cause they would have to get everybody together in one huge space. And obviously that's not possible, even with computers. And not only that, they'd have to get all the people who ever lived, not just the ones now. So they got no proof. They got nothin'.

(Season 3, Episode 2, "Proshai, Livushka")

If He Didn't Laugh,
It Wouldn't Be Tao!

When a wise person hears Tao,
He practices it diligently.
When an average person hears Tao,
He practices it sometimes,
And just as often ignores it.
When an inferior person hears Tao,
He roars with laughter.
If he didn't laugh,
It wouldn't be Tao!

Tao Te Ching ☯ 41

FATHER PHIL: Hey Tony, you like crème anglaise?

TONY: Hey, you bless it, I'll eat it.

(Season 1, Episode 1, "Pilot")

DR. MELFI: When's the last time you had a prostate exam?

TONY: Hey, I don't even let anyone wag their finger in my face.

(Season 1, Episode 6, "Pax Soprana")

JUNIOR: Federal Marshall is so far up my ass, I can taste Brylcream.

(Season 2, Episode 3, "Toodle-Fucking-Oo")

RALPH: Mrs. Custer grabs the artist. "Oh! I tell you I want a painting commemoratin' my husband's last thoughts. You give me cows with halos and Indians makin' love?" "Mrs. Custer," he says, "Those are your husband's last thoughts." "Holy cow . . . look at all those fuckin' Indians."

(Season 3, Episode 6, "University")

TONY: How's your family doin', you know, since the tragedy with your dad?

BACALA: Rough on my mother.

TONY: Well . . . How old is she now?

BACALA: She's sixty-nine. Mom really went downhill after the World Trade Center. You know, Quasimodo predicted all this.

TONY: Who did what?

BACALA: All these problems. The Middle East, the end of the world.

TONY: Nostradamus. Quasimodo's the Hunchback of Notre Dame.

BACALA: Oh, right. Notredamus.

TONY: Nostradamus, and Notre Dame. It's two different things completely.

BACALA: It's interesting though they'd be so similar, isn't it? And I always thought, okay. Hunchback of Notre Dame. You also got your quarterback and your halfback of Notre Dame.

TONY: One's a fuckin' cathedral.

BACALA: Obviously, I know, I'm just sayin'. It's interesting the coincidence. What, you gonna tell me you never pondered that? The back thing with Notre Dame?

(Season 4, Episode 1, "For All Debts Public and Private")

CHRISTOPHER: This is fuckin' great, I mean, I know I'm just the acting, but still . . .

SILVIO: It's a big responsibility, Chrissy.

CHRISTOPHER: Hey, I got it covered. First thing I'm doin', is gettin' wings in my hair. You know, like Paulie.

(Season 4, Episode 2, "No-Show")

CHRISTOPHER: Ho! What the fuck?!

ADRIANA: I saw what you did. What'd you think? You were gonna fuck the two of us?! You and those fuckin' videos!

CHRISTOPHER: She came onto me! She took my hand, she was rubbin' it on herself.

ADRIANA: Bullshit.

CHRISTOPHER: Yeah? How about right before you came over? She was tellin' me where she buys her pants. Her fuckin' underwear and shit. Fuckin' Bebe's. Like I give a fuck.

ADRIANA: Thought you said she was gay.

CHRISTOPHER: Who knows what her problem is? Broad like her'll fuck a snake. Use your head, huh? What do I want with that skank when I got you?

ADRIANA: You were sayin' she had a nice ass.

CHRISTOPHER: I was tryin' to say somethin' positive 'cause she's your friend.

(Season 4, Episode 2, "No-Show")

SILVIO: It's all right. You had a good run, T. You held the dice for quite a while.

TONY: Look at this operation. Whenever I'm in one of these places I remember that my grandmother was part Fugahwe. Maybe I should do somethin' about it.

SILVIO: Bullshit.

TONY: It's true. She was. They were a nomadic tribe and they'd wander around, they'd get lost and they'd go 'We're the Fugahwe?'

(Season 4, Episode 3, "Christopher")

TONY: Just wanna ask you if it's possible for a man to go out with a woman without really doin' anything with 'em.

DR. MELFI: You'll have to be more specific.

TONY: He likes them to hurt him. Now that's it. And then he goes and he . . . takes care of himself, his own needs.

DR. MELFI: He sounds like a textbook masochist.

TONY: Like S & M.

DR. MELFI: The M part, yes.

TONY: I thought all that stuff was just like a run-up to the act.

DR. MELFI: That's the case for many people. But not for people with paraphilias. For them, receiving pain, being humiliated becomes in and of itself, the sexual release. Like many other things we believe it's rooted in childhood. We can continue this next week.

TONY: Just one more second. I received regular beatin's when I was a kid, but I'm not goin' around lookin' for some woman to hook up jumper cables to my private parts.

DR. MELFI: It's not a simple one-to-one. More than likely he had a controlling and punishing mother. She loved him but showed it only in connection with some sort of . . . violent or abusive act.

TONY: Is everything about everybody really about their mothers? All right, about the other thing. For a guy like that, he's goin' out with a woman, he could technically not have penisary contact with her volvo.

DR. MELFI: It sounds like you're asking me for personal information I really can't give you.

(Season 4, Episode 8, "Mergers and Acquisitions")

There Is No Greater Misfortune

There is no greater misfortune
Than underestimating your opponent.

Tao Te Ching ☯ 69

PAULIE: Look, pal, I don't think you quite understand.

COACH: Oh, I understand, all right, only too well. You tell your friends I know all about them.

PAULIE: If you did, you'd do what they want.

COACH: Is that a threat? How quickly things change. Let me tell you something, Guido . . .

PAULIE: My name is Clarence.

(Season 1, Episode 9, "Boca")

JO JO: We're goin' to Vegas next month. I already lined up childcare for Frances Albert, so, I don't wanna hear it.

MIKEY: Forget it, somethin's come up.

JO JO: Somethin' always comes up.

MIKEY: This is a *good* something.

JO JO: Hope it means more money 'cause I need a new car.

MIKEY: Trust me . . . if this goes down, you're gonna have a new car, and then some.

JO JO: Can you tell me? Oh, come on, Mikey! Tell me.

MIKEY: Mmm-mmm.

JO JO: Come on, please?

MIKEY: I may be gettin' bumped up, a notch or two! Tony Soprano's on his way out, and I mean as in *forever*!

JO JO: Oh, my God! He's goin' to jail?

MIKEY: No, the other forever!

(Season 1, Episode 11, "Nobody Knows Anything")

CUBITOSO: Boy, we've had every one of Tony's phones bugged for four years. But the guy says less than Harpo Marx.

(Season 3, Episode 1, "Mr. Ruggerio's Neighborhood")

SAPINSLY: Help you?

TONY: Hi, how ya doing? I'm Tony Soprano. I was here with my wife the other day with Virginia Lupo.

SAPINSLY: Oh, right, right. Alan Sapinsly.

TONY: How are ya?

SAPINSLY: So, what do you think?

TONY: She says those other people are gonna go through with it. I was gonna go talk to you frankly, after I took another look at the place.

SAPINSLY: The whole thing is so galling because I don't think they're going to qualify for financing and we gave them this God-awful ninety-day escrow—my wife's doing . . . she liked Mrs. Kim.

TONY: I can do fifteen days. Shortest allowable by law.

SAPINSLY: [RE: THE OCEAN] Never tire of painting this. You'd be coming in with cash, right?

TONY: Yeah.

SAPINSLY: Fuck this. [INTO PHONE] Dr. Kim? Hey, Alan Sapinsly. It's not, huh? Well, we've got serious problems . . . On the house . . . Sure . . . [TO TONY] He's going into surgery. Doesn't want to talk there in the prep room. [INTO PHONE] Yes, I'm here. So look, what does your lender say? . . . Jesus, Doctor . . . Well, I take almost no comfort from those words. And were I you, I wouldn't either . . . I'm aware we have a contract in place. Doctor, please, I'm an attorney. Look, Cho-sun . . . no wait, you're not listening. Simply stated, I want the chance to sell to a more qualified buyer, if I can find one at this late date . . . What? Actually, it's very simp . . . Wait, do you want to do all the talking and I'll just stand here? Thank you. You call Virginia Lupo, she calls the bank, you get your deposit back . . . Your wife's a grown woman, she'll adjust . . . Look, Doctor Kim, I spent ten years as a litigator. Buy this property, I'll make your life a misery. I can tort you into the poorhouse. I've got an overseas call. Well, think it over. You have Virginia's number. [TO TONY] Who knows? We'll see.

TONY: I wouldn't want to be the patient he's gonna operate on.

SAPINSLY: Let's hold a good thought?

(Season 4, Episode 13, "Whitecaps")

SAPINSLY: Tony? Alan Sapinsly.

TONY: What?

SAPINSLY: I hadn't heard from you. My partners and I have decided to let you out of your obligation.

TONY: Well, I want my two hundred grand by the end of the week.

SAPINSLY: As to that, I'm not rescinding the deposit. That's what they're for, to hold parties to agreements. If you want to make me an offer . . .

TONY: No, I think I'll buy the house. My family has parties. Till four, five in the morning.

SAPINSLY: I can show damages and I'm being generous in not bringing action to enforce the sale.

TONY: Damages? They haven't started yet.

SAPINSLY: Listen to me. There's a paper trail to our dispute and Virginia Lupo's a witness. A hair on my head gets mussed, the authorities are gonna know just where to come knocking.

TONY: Alan, you misread me entirely. You must think I'm a fuckin' thug.

SAPINSLY: Just be forewarned. You're not getting your deposit back.

(Season 4, Episode 13, "Whitecaps")

A Man of Violence

A man of violence will come to a violent end.

Tao Te Ching ☯ 42

RICHIE: [COMPLAINING ABOUT HIS SON]) He carries my name. Richard. Fuckin' disgraziat'. My nephew Jackie . . . why couldn't I have a son like that?

JANICE: You know, you came home with a fuckin' attitude today. God, you know, I've been in this house cookin' your fuckin' dinner . . . and taking care of that fuckin' black hole upstairs all day!

RICHIE: Keep your voice down, she hears everything.

JANICE: Not tonight. I gave her two Nembutols because I thought maybe we'd like to have sex. But not likely.

RICHIE: Put my fuckin' dinner on the table and keep your mouth shut.

JANICE: No, you shut up. What, just because he's a ballroom dancer you think your son is gay. And what if he was gay, what difference does it make? [RICHIE PUNCHES HER IN THE FACE.] Uh! Oh. Fuck . . .

RICHIE: What are you looking at? You gonna cry now? Get the fuck outta here. I'm in no mood for your—[JANICE SHOOTS HIM IN THE CHEST] Shit.

⊕ ⊕ ⊕ ⊕ ⊕

TONY: [INTO PHONE] Hello?

JANICE: [OVER PHONE, CRYING] Tony? I need you. I need you to come over now. Okay?

TONY: Whatsa matter? Is it Ma?

JANICE: No, no . . .

TONY: Tell me what happened.

JANICE: No, I– I– I can't . . . say . . .

TONY: What do you mean, you can't say?

JANICE: No, I can't say now. Think. Think a minute, okay?

TONY: All right, just stay right there! I'm gonna be right over! [TO CARMELA] It's Janice.

⊕ ⊕ ⊕ ⊕ ⊕

TONY: Janice.

JANICE: Ton'? Ton', he hit me, it was an accident. [WHISPERS TO RICHIE'S BODY] Baby, baby, baby, baby . . .

TONY: Where's Ma?

JANICE: Upstairs. Out. She took two Nembutols.

TONY: Ma?

JANICE: I didn't mean it, Tony. I didn't mean it.

TONY: Where's the gun?

JANICE: In the cabinet.

TONY: If anybody calls this in, if there's any shit about this, you don't gotta talk to anybody.

(Season 2, Episode 12, "The Knight in White Satin Armor")

JUNIOR: What's with you? All day, Gloomy Gus.

BACALA: Sorry, it's just . . . it's my father.

JUNIOR: He's a tough man, he'll beat the fuckin' thing.

BACALA: It's not the cancer, it's Tony.

JUNIOR: Tony? Well, what about him? Stop speakin' in anagrams.

BACALA: He okayed my dad to do the hit on Mustang Sally.

JUNIOR: Well, the prick put that Spatafore kid in a coma.

BACALA: Fuck Sally, I'm worried about my father. He can't do this. He's been retired for seven years.

JUNIOR: What's this we're in, the Navy?

(Season 3, Episode 5, "Another Toothpick")

CARMELA: Let me tell you something. Or you can watch the fucking news. Everything comes to an end.

(Season 4, Episode 1, "For All Debts Public and Private")

TONY: So, how's your love life?

JANICE: Why don't you mind your goddamn business?

TONY: I don't know, it kinda feels like it is my business considerin' I had to haul your last boyfriend outta your kitchen . . . in a Hefty bag.

(Season 4, Episode 2, "No-Show")

PUSSY: Sure you wanna go out today, T? Just gettin' over the trots.

TONY: Time and tide wait for no man, right? Got a decent displacement for its size. Mill puts out about 700 horsepower.

PUSSY: Beautiful boat, Tony.

PAULIE: I've been waitin' forty minutes! The Cuban had to go see the harbor master. But uh, we're free to give it a spin. Come on, Puss'.

[PUSSY STANDS LOOKING APPREHENSIVE]

⊕ ⊕ ⊕ ⊕ ⊕

TONY: Why you makin' me do this, you fat fuckin' miserable piece of shit?

PUSSY: What, Tony? What?

TONY: When did they flip you? Tell me. Don't lie.

PUSSY: Flip! Who? What? . . . They had me, Tony. I was goin' away for pushin' H.

TONY: How long?

PUSSY: Thirty to life. Had no choice.

TONY: How long? How much do they know?

PUSSY: A year and a half. No, less.

SILVIO: A year and a fuckin' half you been runnin' your own fuckin' gossip column?

PAULIE: Motherfucker!

PUSSY: Let me explain. I fed them bullshit. Nothin'! Whatchamacallit, disinformation. So I could live. Keep earnin' on any subsistence level whatsoever. I would do nothin', Tony. Nothin' to put you in harm's way! All of yous!

TONY: That's how they got tipped off about the Bevilaqua hit, huh? 'Cause you did nothin'.

PUSSY: On my mother's eyes, that wasn't me! Little things! Picayune shit!

TONY: Be specific.

PUSSY: They know about the callin' cards.

PAULIE: I'm not in that. What else?

PUSSY: That's it. That is . . . recently.

TONY: What not recently?

PUSSY: I'm thinkin'. The other shit. None of it amounted to anything. I've been careful, I got this down. I'm mind-fuckin' these donkeys like you wouldn't believe!

TONY: Webistics? Oh, Jesus Christ.

PUSSY: But mostly I talked up the Scatino bust out. Nothin' federal that'll link you, Tony. They need serial numbers. I'm tellin' you. This disinformation shit is an effective technique! It's a friggin' ace!

TONY: What's the matter with you?

SILVIO: It's this fuckin' . . . swell.

TONY: I got food poisonin' and you don't see me gettin' all fucked up.

SILVIO: Don't yell at me!

TONY: I'll fuckin' yell at you, you don't like it?!

PUSSY: We got any good tequila? That acupuncturist down in Puerto Rico? Twenty-six. I'll tell you, this broad . . . Her ass was the second comin'. Never wore panties. Brushed her teeth with this shit. Every night she'd drink me under the fuckin' table. And I'd eat her out while I was down there. Ahhh.

TONY: Hey, Puss . . . she even really exist?

SILVIO: Fucked up.

PUSSY: Not in the face, okay? Give me that. Huh? Keep my eyes.

PAULIE: You were like a brother to me.

TONY: To all of us.

PUSSY: Yeah. I'm startin' to feel it now, too. My inner ear balance is off. Jesus Christ. I gotta sit down. I feel like I can't stand. Is that okay, Tony? That I sit?

TONY: Get the weights.

(Season 2, Episode 13, "Funhouse")

Söpranos

LIST OF EPISODES AND WRITERS

#101, Pilot: David Chase

#102, "46 Long": David Chase

#103, "Denial, Anger, Acceptance": Mark Saraceni

#104, "Meadowlands": Jason Cahill

#105, "College": James Manos, Jr. and David Chase

#106, "Pax Soprana": Frank Renzulli

#107, "Down Neck": Mitchell Burgess & Robin Green

#108, "The Legend of Tennessee Moltisanti": Frank Renzulli and David Chase

#109, "Boca": Jason Cahill and Mitchell Burgess & Robin Green

#110, "A Hit Is a Hit": Joe Bosso and Frank Renzulli

#111, "Nobody Knows Anything": Frank Renzulli

#112, "Isabella": Robin Green & Mitchell Burgess

#113, "I Dream of Jeannie Cusamano": David Chase

#201, "Guy Walks into a Psychiatrist's Office…": Jason Cahill

#202, "Do Not Resuscitate": Robin Green & Mitchell Burgess and Frank Renzulli

#203, "Toodle-Fucking-Oo": Frank Renzulli

#204, "Commendatori": David Chase

#205, "Big Girls Don't Cry": Terence Winter

#206, "The Happy Wanderer": Frank Renzulli

#207, "D-Girl": Todd A. Kessler

#208, "Full Leather Jacket": Robin Green & Mitchell Burgess

#209, "From Where to Eternity": Michael Imperioli

#210, "Bust Out": Frank Renzulli and Robin Green & Mitchell Burgess

#211, "House Arrest": Terence Winter

#212, "The Knight in White Satin Armor": Robin Green & Mitchell Burgess

#213, "Fun House": David Chase and Todd A. Kessler

#301, "Mr. Ruggerio's Neighborhood": David Chase

#302, "Proshai, Livushka": David Chase

#303, "Fortunate Son": Todd A. Kessler

#304, "Employee of the Month": Robin Green & Mitchell Burgess

#305, "Another Toothpick": Terence Winter

#306, "University": Teleplay by Terence Winter and Salvatore J. Stabile. Story by David Chase & Terence Winter & Todd A. Kessler and Robin Green & Mitchell Burgess

#307, "Second Opinion": Lawrence Konner

#308, "He Is Risen": Robin Green & Mitchell Burgess and Todd A. Kessler

#309, "The Telltale Moozadell'": Michael Imperioli

#310, "...To Save Us All from Satan's Power...": Robin Green & Mitchell Burgess

#311, "Pine Barrens": Teleplay by Terence Winter. Story by Tim Van Patten & Terence Winter

#312, "Amour Fou": Teleplay by Frank Renzulli. Story by David Chase

#313, "The Army of One": David Chase & Lawrence Konner

#401, "For All Debts Public and Private": David Chase

#402, "No-Show": Terence Winter and David Chase

#403, "Christopher": Teleplay by Michael Imperioli. Story by Michael Imperioli and Maria Laurino

#404, "The Weight": Terence Winter

#405, "Pie-O-My": Robin Green & Mitchell Burgess

#406, "Everybody Hurts": Michael Imperioli

#407, "Watching Too Much Television": Teleplay by Terence Winter and Nick Santora. Story by David Chase & Robin Green & Mitchell Burgess & Terence Winter

#408, "Mergers and Acquisitions": Teleplay by Lawrence Konner. Story by David Chase & Robin Green & Mitchell Burgess & Terence Winter

#409, "Whoever Did This": Robin Green & Mitchell Burgess

#410, "The Strong, Silent Type": Teleplay by Terence Winter and Robin Green & Mitchell Burgess. Story by David Chase

#411, "Calling All Cars": Teleplay by David Chase & Robin Green & Mitchell Burgess and David Flebotte. Story by David Chase & Robin Green & Mitchell Burgess & Terence Winter

#412, "Eloise": Terence Winter

#413, "Whitecaps": Robin Green & Mitchell Burgess and David Chase

A Note on the Translations

There are more than a hundred translations of the *Tao Te Ching* into English. These range from the literal to the impressionistic, in which the translator tries to reproduce the meaning of the original work for a contemporary reader.

The chapters of *The Tao of Bada Bing!* begin with a quotation from the *Tao Te Ching*, drawn from one of four different and excellent translations. We list each book below, accompanied by copyright information, a list of the chapters in *The Tao of Bada Bing!* that feature quotations from that particular translation, and the chapter number of the quotations in the *Tao Te Ching*.

TRANSLATIONS OF THE *TAO TE CHING*

TAO TE CHING by Lao Tzu
Translated by Stephen Mitchell.
Translation copyright © 1988 by Stephen Mitchell.
Reprinted by permission of HarperCollins (ISBN 0-06-081245-1).

> Written in the Blood (51)
> Those Who Know (56)
> If a Country Is Governed Wisely (80)
> Do You Have the Patience to Wait? (15)
> Act without Doing (63)
> Not Knowing Is True Knowledge (71)
> There Is No Greater Misfortune (69)

THE TAO TE CHING OF LAO TZU
Translated by Brian Browne Walker.
Translation copyright © 1995 by Brian Browne Walker.
Reprinted by permission of St. Martin's Press, LLC (ISBN 0-312-13190-9).

> My Sustenance Comes from the Mother (20)
> Only One in Ten (50)
> A Man Who Justifies His Actions (24)